The legal way to protect your
Products, Business and Innovations

INTE  L
PRO

The John & Kernick Guide

Compiled and edited by
Mike von Seidel

JONATHAN BALL PUBLISHERS
JOHANNESBURG

Published by
JONATHAN BALL PUBLISHERS (PTY) LTD
P O Box 33977
Jeppestown 2043

ISBN 1 86842 064 7

Design by Michael Barnett, Johannesburg
Typesetting and reproduction of text by Book Productions, Pretoria
Reproduction of cover by Ince (Pty) Ltd, Johannesburg
Printed and bound by National Book Printers, Drukkery Street, Goodwood, Western Cape

INTELLECTUAL PROPERTY

Contents

Preface   *7*

Acknowledgements   *8*

Introduction and Overview   *9*

1 Patents   *15*

2 How to Read a Patent Specification   *31*

3 Know-how   *37*

4 Trade Marks   *40*

5 The Protection of Trading Names   *51*

6 Registered Designs   *55*

7 Unlawful Competition and Restraints of Trade   *61*

8 Product Liability and Product Warranties   *68*

9 Copyright   *73*

10 The Effect of the Internet on Intellectual
Property Rights   *85*

11 Counterfeit Goods   *90*

12 Plant Breeders' Rights   *96*

13 Licences   *98*

14 Franchising   *106*

15 Managing and Using Intellectual Property
Assets   *111*

16 The Law of Contract   *122*

Index   *128*

Preface

It has always been a mission of John & Kernick to educate clients in the area of intellectual property law. Our experience over 75 years in this area shows that there is generally considerable ignorance about intellectual property laws – particularly about ways in which measures such as patents, registered designs and trade marks can protect business interests and innovations. It being time consuming to educate clients on a one-to-one basis, it made sense to provide the necessary basic knowledge in a booklet. This was done first in 1987, in an edition put together by John & Kernick partners, Peter James and Paul Novellie. In its green cover this soon became fondly known as 'the green book'. When stocks were exhausted, I took on the job of producing a greatly expanded edition in 1991, and went on to produce three further editions, each appropriately expanded and updated, in 1993, 1994 and 1996.

The usefulness and popularity of the book among our own clientele makes it viable to publish the information we have put together for the benefit of a wider public. Indeed this new edition, substantially expanded, serves as a comprehensive guide to intellectual property law – not only for the business person, but also for the attorney not specialising in intellectual property. We are glad to offer this comprehensive new edition information and guidance to enable you to use intellectual property laws to the best advantage of your business.

Mike von Seidel
JOHN & KERNICK
Johannesburg 1998

Acknowledgements

In compiling and editing this handbook I wish to acknowledge with heartfelt thanks the specialist contributions and comment that I have received from my colleagues – qualified staff and partners of the intellectual property law firm, John & Kernick. I am also indebted to my darling wife, Stella, who through her desktop publishing business, Composed Communications cc, tirelessly created the previous four editions of the book and assisted me with the present edition.

Introduction and Overview

Intellectual property rights – which can take the form of trade marks, copyright, designs, patents, and so on – are becoming increasingly visible in the South African commercial world. The success of a business often depends to a substantial extent on preventing others – or being entitled to prevent them – from copying products, or from selling the systems or the style of the business.

South Africa's national business news has focused in recent years on piracy of products, software and famous trade marks; theft of confidential information; restraints of trade for employees and managers; and disputes over the ownership of copyright in computer programs. The patent rights of disposable nappies for babies have been in the news, as have been plant breeders' rights – which protect a Californian grape cultivar now becoming popular in South Africa. Companies and individuals are discovering how various intellectual property rights can promote their business interests – or how the intellectual property rights of others can hamper their efforts. Because of their wide ranging effects, it is thus important for people to have a basic understanding of what intellectual property rights are.

The main objective of this book is to inform you of the various types of intellectual property rights that can be used to protect innovations and business. Equally important, the purpose is to enable you to distinguish these rights from each other. A third objective of the book is to give you an idea of how to use these rights, and which of the types of rights apply in different circumstances. Tax considerations can also be relevant

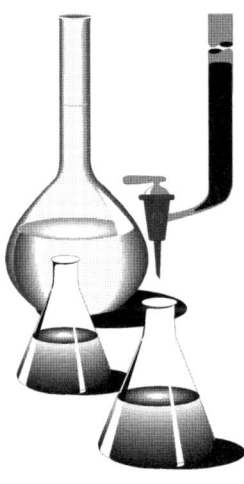

**THE SCOPE OF
INTELLECTUAL
PROPERTY LAW**

when using intellectual property rights, and these are also briefly dealt with.

The information given in this book is essentially introductory, and should not be treated as comprehensive. You are strongly advised to consult a patent or trade mark attorney or other intellectual property law specialist before publishing or using any new material – not only because of possible changes to the various laws, but also because of the complexity of intellectual property law, and the possibility of permanently losing your rights if you don't take appropriate action before publishing an innovation or a work.

The term 'intellectual property' covers all forms of rights (generally termed proprietary rights) that enable a person or company to prevent others from conduct which would give them an unfair trade advantage. This can include manufacturing or marketing commercial products that have a particular construction, appearance, intellectual content, marketing name, style or get-up.

Intellectual property is divided into a number of different categories. Each category relates to a different aspect of an owner's manufacturing, compiling, marketing or commercial use of his proprietary rights. Thus, a number of different forms of protection are available. An owner may sell his proprietary rights (by way of assignment); or hire out his proprietary rights (generally by way of a licence contract), usually in return for some form of payment, often a royalty. A single commercial process or product can be the subject of a number of different forms of protection. To take a computer as an example, each of the following features could be protected as intellectual property:

• patents for the hardware;
• registered designs for the shape or style of the casing;
• trade marks;
• copyright in respect of the software and manuals; and
• rights afforded by unlawful competition.

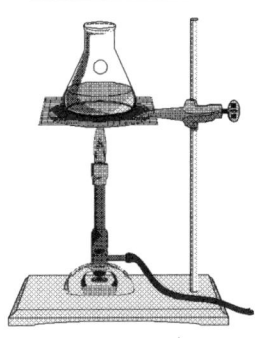

In some instances, it may be expedient to use a company or close corporation to hold, exercise or defend intellectual property rights and the effect of the names or trading styles of such companies or close corporations can be enhanced or diluted by proper selection of the name of trade marks used for other appropriate products or services.

Patents

The way in which a process is carried out, or the basis, or principle of operation of a product or machine, can be protected by means of a patent. Patents are granted for inventions which have not been previously known, and which differ adequately from what was previously done along the same lines. Some countries provide two different forms of patents, namely, a full patent, and a utility model or petty patent. A full patent is granted for distinctly ingenious inventions and a petty patent is usually granted for somewhat less ingenious inventions. South Africa has only a single form of patent at present. Patents are dealt with in Chapter 1. Interpreting a patent specification, which can be extremely important, is dealt with in Chapter 2.

Know-how

'Know-how' generally refers to secret technology, and usually relates to processes. Secret technology is not always patentable. However, know-how is a form of intellectual property, and can be licensed to others in return for payment. This is often a lump sum plus a royalty. Know-how maintains its value only for so long as it is secret (that is, while it is not freely available to others). It is dealt with in Chapter 3.

Trade marks

The name or logo attached to an article for marketing, or to a service rendered – and in fact, even the way a product or part of it looks, its shape, configuration, colour, pattern or ornamentation (for example, the grille of a BMW or Mercedes Benz, or the shape of a

specialised container) – can be registered as a trade mark. An owner of a trade mark can market any number of products under the same trade mark (usually referred to as 'branding'), and can prevent others from using it in relation to similar goods or services. Trade marks must be sufficiently different from prior trade marks in order to be registered. Trade marks are dealt with in Chapter 4.

In order to be fully effective, trade marks must be protected from being included in a company or close corporation name, which could detract from the value of the trade mark. This aspect is dealt with in Chapter 5 under the title 'The protection of trading names'.

Piracy and counterfeiting

This is generally a transgression of the trade mark and unlawful competition categories. It arises when articles, their get-up and packaging are closely copied, and requires some special comment, which is given in Chapter 11.

Registered designs

The visual, or as it is generally termed aesthetic, appearance of an article may be protected by a form of registered design, provided that it is new in comparison to anything previously known on articles of a similar nature. Such designs are termed aesthetic designs, and are judged solely by the eye.

Functional aspects, and more particularly the shape of an article, cannot be covered by the registration of aesthetic design, but the South African Designs Act does provide for the separate registration of functional designs.

Registered designs are dealt with in Chapter 6.

Unlawful competition

It is sometimes possible to prevent the manufacture and marketing of articles, or the carrying out of a service by others, in the absence of a patent, registered design or registered trade mark, under a category of intellectual property law – developed by the courts in the form of common law – known as unlawful competition.

The scope and content of this category of intellectual property law will probably change with time as the courts are faced with different situations. At present, this category covers three main areas. It enables a person or company to prevent others from marketing products, or carrying out a service, in a manner which confuses them with those of the person or company having established rights. This is generally termed passing-off. A person or company may also prevent an employee from using a former employer's secret information. Thirdly, this category of intellectual property law can be used generally to prevent competition in an unlawful manner. The scope of application of unlawful competition is open-ended. It is dealt with in Chapter 8.

Product liability and product warranties

Product liability is closely allied to unlawful competition. It deals with the responsibilities of a manufacturer or distributor of a product which turns out to have a harmful effect on the property or person of others. This law also has its roots in common law, and is based on ancient Roman law. Product liability is dealt with in Chapter 9, which also deals with a manufacturer or distributor's responsibilities consequent on product warranties, either express or implied by common law.

Copyright

Artistic works and other works containing intellectual content such as literary works, music, cinematographic films, sound recordings, drawings (including engineering drawings), plans, computer programs, pictures of all forms, and numerous other two- and three-dimensional articles having intellectual content, are covered by copyright.

Copyright simply means the right not to be copied. It thus enables the copyright owner to prevent others from copying an original work to any substantial extent. Copyright exists automatically and no steps need be taken in South Africa to register it, although in the

exclusive case of video recordings and cinematographic films, the copyright can be registered. Copyright is dealt with in Chapter 10.

The Internet
The Internet, a feature of the information technology highway, and its effect on intellectual property rights – in particular, trade marks and copyright – is briefly dealt with in Chapter 11.

Plants
Protection is available for new varieties of plants. They can be protected in terms of the Plant Breeders' Rights Act and are specifically excluded from being made the subject of a patent. Chapter 12 deals briefly with this category of intellectual property law.

Licences
As indicated above, all forms of intellectual property mentioned can be licensed to others, and accordingly a short section covering licences is found in Chapter 13.

Franchising
Franchising is simply a particular form of licensing, but because of its highly developed and specialised nature, and also its importance in the business community, it is dealt with separately in Chapter 14.

Managing the portfolio
Chapter 15 gives a brief commentary on the procurement and management of an intellectual property portfolio as well as a checklist of matters that should be attended to before an innovation is publicised or implemented.

Contracts
Because many of the rights discussed in this book are exercised under a contract of licence, or involve other contracts, the general principles of contract are briefly covered in Chapter 16.

1   Patents

The granting of patents in the Republic of South Africa is governed by the Patents Act of 1978 (as amended) and the Regulations under it. The law in force prior to 1978 controls only a few patents applied for before 1 January 1979, which had their terms extended. The information given here relates almost exclusively to the present Act.

WHAT IS A PATENT?

A patent is a monopoly or an exclusive right granted for a specific period of time by the State to an inventor, or to another person or people entitled to the relevant invention, in exchange for a full disclosure of the invention to the public. This monopoly entitles a patent holder to prevent others, within the territory of the State, from using the invention in any practical manner for the duration of the patent. After expiry of the period members of the public are free to use the invention. The term 'use of an invention' is broad, but essentially the intention is to allow the patentee to enjoy any profit or advantage that the invention affords. As a patent is not enforced by the State automatically, the patent holder must enforce the patent through the appropriate courts.

The full disclosure of the invention to the public is made in a patent specification which includes written claims to stake out the extent of the monopoly claimed. The specification is therefore the equivalent of a title deed and must be properly drafted. It is in this regard that the advice and assistance of a patent attorney or agent is generally necessary. Reading and interpreting a patent specification is crucial and is thus dealt with separately in Chapter 2.

* Your patent attorney is not necessarily skilled in the art. He needs all possible input from the inventor.

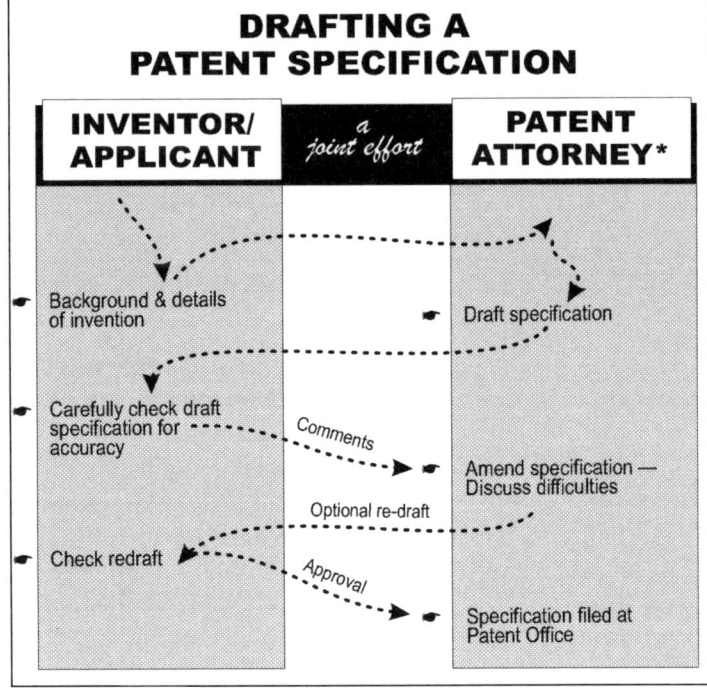

DRAFTING A PATENT SPECIFICATION

INVENTOR/ APPLICANT	*a joint effort*	**PATENT ATTORNEY***

Background & details of invention → Draft specification

Carefully check draft specification for accuracy ····· *Comments* → Amend specification — Discuss difficulties

Optional re-draft

Check redraft ····· *Approval* → Specification filed at Patent Office

A patent is property and may be sold (by way of assignment) or licensed for use by others (generally effected by way of a licence contract).

WHAT IS PATENTABLE?

Generally, any invention in the form of an apparatus, an article, device, method or process is patentable if it fulfills three basic requirements: it must be novel; of some practical use; and inventive. These characteristics are discussed more fully below. In this context, the word 'invention' relates to the way in which an apparatus, article or method operates, irrespective of its appearance or exact physical form. A patent, therefore, covers a principle of operation or construction.

An idea, as such, is not patentable, but can often be reduced to one of the forms of invention mentioned above which are patentable. The Patents Act stipulates that – irrespective of whether or not they fulfill the three requirements for patentability – the following are not patentable:

- mathematical methods;
- aesthetic creations (for instance, fashion designs, motor vehicle designs, etc);
- architectural designs;
- schemes, for example, investment or insurance schemes;
- business methods (such as credit or stock control);
- rules for playing games (the games equipment may be patentable);
- computer programs; and
- scientific theories (for example, Einstein's theory of relativity).

THE THREE REQUIREMENTS FOR PATENTABILITY

Novelty

The invention must be new. This means that it must not have been made available to the public anywhere in the world – by word of mouth, by use, in any printed publication, or in any other way – before a first application is made for a patent. To destroy novelty, however, a description of the invention must have been made in sufficient detail to enable it to be properly understood by a person familiar with the relevant technology. The invention must also not have been the subject of secret commercial use in South Africa prior to the date on which the first patent application is made.

Left:
Patent drawing of a heat exchanger by Krupp Koppers GmbH

Right:
Patent drawing of a flotation machine by Yakutsky Nauchno-Issledovatelsky I Proekiny Institut Almazaodobyvajuschei Promyshlnnotsi

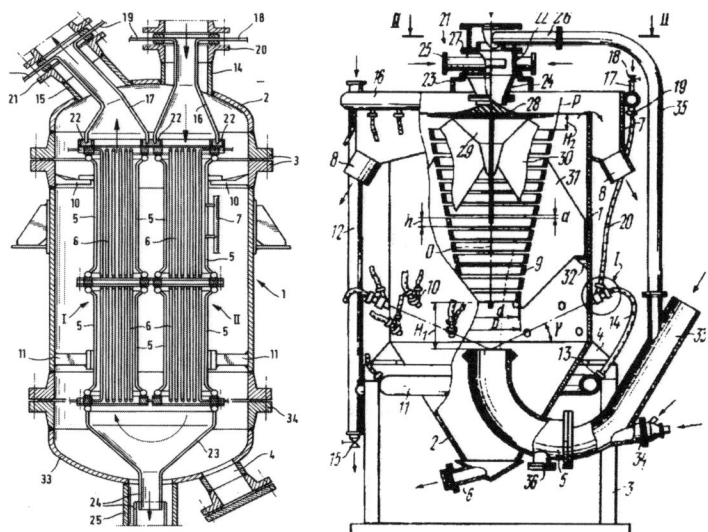

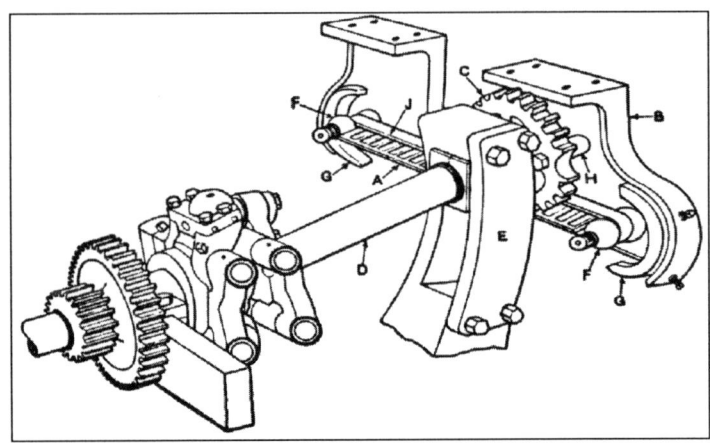

This type of novelty is known as absolute novelty. It is difficult to establish whether or not an invention is in fact new, but novelty may be assessed by carrying out searches through existing printed publications that include previously published patent specifications. However, because of the time and cost involved in conducting searches, it is often preferable to file a patent application immediately. This allows for the invention to be technically or practically tested, and for market research to be carried out, before incurring the costs of searches. At the same time the patentability of the invention is preserved.

However, it is highly desirable to have a search carried out in instances where patents in foreign countries are required, as foreign patent applications are costly and the possibility of obtaining strong patents should be properly assessed. (Patent searches and foreign patent applications are dealt with further below.)

The requirement that an invention be new makes it essential to keep the invention secret before an application for a patent is made. The invention could be disclosed to others in confidence, but preferably only after a written secrecy agreement has been signed.

Utility

The invention must be useful on a practical level. The Patents Act requires that, for an invention to be patentable, it must be capable of being applied in trade, industry or agriculture.

Inventiveness

The invention must be inventive – that is, it must not be so similar to what was available or used previously that it required little or no ingenuity to make the invention. Generally, the expressions 'obvious' or 'lack of inventive step' are used to indicate that this requirement is not fulfilled. For example, it would be obvious to make an article that was previously made exclusively of metal in a plastic material, if there were no special and unforseeable advantages, even if the article had never previously been made, or had never been described as having been proposed or made, in plastic.

TYPES OF PATENT SEARCHES

There are three broad categories of patent searches: the name index search; the 'family' search; and the subject matter search. Name index and subject matter searches can be conducted through the records of the South African or any other national patent office. These records relate only to the relevant national patents and applications. Searches done as a precaution against infringement of someone else's patent rights must generally be carried out in the relevant country or countries.

International patent databases are available for conducting on-line name index, family and subject matter searches. Database searches have the advantage of being less costly than instructing foreign associates to conduct a search. More importantly, results can be obtained in a very short time: a database search can be done and the results made available within days. The drawback is that database records only go back to about 1968, and the search is based on catchwords which are sometimes difficult to determine. Thus database searches are usually regarded as preparatory or exploratory and are particularly useful as information searches.

More extensive – and more expensive – international searches are also available. They are, in fact, recommended where costly foreign patent applications

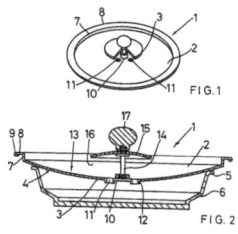

Patent drawing of lid
for a cooking utensil
by H M Henderson

are to be filed. These searches are best chosen according to individual requirements, the nature of the invention, and the countries in which protection is to be considered.

Name index search

A name index search is conducted through patent records to determine details of patents or patent applications held by specific inventors, applicants for patents and patentees.

This type of search can be commissioned when the searcher suspects that a business rival has an invention and wants to check whether it has been patented. It is also used when someone wishes to purchase a company and wants to check on its intellectual property assets. Thirdly, it can be done in order to avoid infringing a particular company's patent rights. In this case, however, it is always strongly advisable to conduct a full infringement search (described under *Subject matter search*, below).

Name index searches are useful where details of an inventor or an applicant are known, or ascertainable with reasonable certainty. Unfortunately this information is not always available. The effectiveness of such searches is reduced by the failure of some patent records, such as the South African records, to reflect changes in ownership of

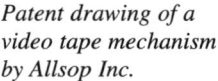

Patent drawing of a
video tape mechanism
by Allsop Inc.

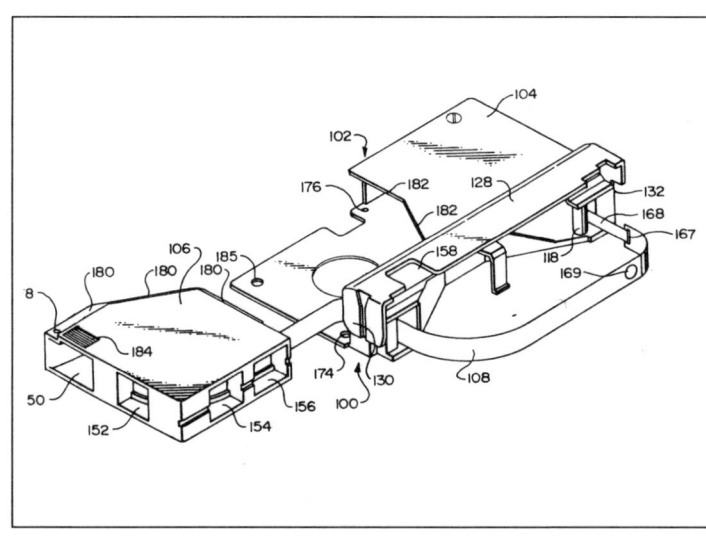

patents after the relevant application for a patent has been made.

'Family' search

This kind of search concerns 'families' of patents – that is, it seeks to gather details of all patents, irrespective of country, which are related to a particular invention. A family search is useful where a person has obtained an article patented overseas and wishes to determine whether the article is protected by a South African patent. Similarly, where a person wishes to export a product, it is useful to establish the extent of foreign patents related to the article.

Subject matter search

This is a search through patent records to find patents disclosing matter of a similar nature. Subject matter searches can also be used for publications other than prior patents. There are three main types of subject matter searches: infringement searches; patentability searches; and information searches.

Patents are classified or grouped according to the nature of the invention. Subject matter searches thus involve a search of all patent records in one or more desired patent classes.

One disadvantage of subject matter searches is that the patent records include details only of granted patents. This is a disadvantage because it can take two years or more from the date on which an application for a patent is filed until the patent is granted. Thus there is a long period during which patent applications will not be detected by searching while at the same time the novelty of an invention may effectively be destroyed.

Infringement search

This is carried out when a person or company wishes to put a product on the market but wants to avoid infringing the patent rights of other parties. The product itself may or may not be patented. The purpose is, therefore, to avoid infringement litigation at a later date; and to avoid

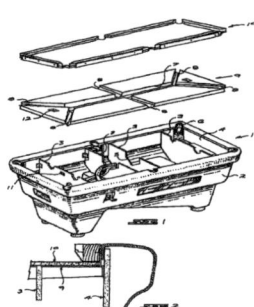

Patent drawing of League Pool Table Technology CC

spending capital and effort on preparations for marketing a product which cannot be freely sold – or at least not without obtaining permission by way of a patent licence from another party.

Patentability search

The purpose of a patentability search is to assess whether or not an invention is patentable, and thus possesses novelty, or to investigate the validity or strength of an existing patent. In essence a patent is granted for an invention which must be new and inventive. The concepts of novelty and validity are evaluated in the light of the prior art. The prior art can be determined by means of a subject matter search. Since the newness of an invention is assessed in the light of all matter which has been disclosed to the public anywhere in the world, a subject matter search limited to patent records does not conclusively indicate the novelty of an invention. Searches through other publications (such as *Chemical Abstracts* or appropriate journals) should also be made in some cases.

Information search

An information search may be carried out in order to establish the existing state of development of any technical area of interest. This type of search is particularly important when a new research and development project is undertaken. The information gathered can be used as a starting point for a new research and development programme, and may also render the research unnecessary by avoiding the well-known error of 're-inventing the wheel'.

The extent of South African records

The records available in South Africa are extremely limited as regards both patentability and information searches. Generally such searches are carried out through substantially more extensive records, such as the patents records of the United States of America, European countries, the European Patent Office and Japan, as well as computer databanks – some of which include other material such as *Chemical Abstracts*.

WHO MAY APPLY FOR A PATENT?

Only the inventor, or another person or body to whom he has assigned his rights to the invention, may apply for a patent in South Africa. There may be more than one inventor in respect of a single invention, so there may be joint owners of a patent application or patent. In the case of an inventor who is an employee, it is often an implied or specified term of employment that inventions be assigned to the employer. In addition, in many cases, the law provides that the employer owns the invention.

On the other hand, irrespective of the terms of an employment contract, no inventor is obliged to assign an invention to an employer if the invention was not made within the scope and course of the inventor's employment. Thus for example a typist in a research organisation who makes an invention important to the business of the organisation cannot be required to assign that invention to the organisation. Similarly, a research worker in a pharmaceutical company who invents a new kitchen gadget will not be obliged to assign it to the organisation although he would be so obliged if the invention related to the work he was employed to do. A research worker also cannot be obliged to assign any relevant invention to that organisation if the invention is made more than a year after employment was terminated.

HOW IS A SOUTH AFRICAN PATENT APPLICATION MADE?

A patent application is made by filing a patent specification, together with the necessary forms and revenue stamps, at the Patent Office in Pretoria. The patent specification, which includes a description of the invention, a description of one or more examples of it, as well as any drawings which may be necessary for a clear understanding of the description, may be either a *provisional* or a *complete* patent specification.

Provisional patent specification

The purpose of filing a provisional specification is primarily to allow the applicant to work on the invention despite any consequent disclosure or commercial use, without losing his rights to patent protection. The result of this is that more and better information can be made available for inclusion in the complete specification when it is filed.

A provisional patent specification, according to the Patents Act, needs to describe the invention only 'fairly'. However, for a variety of reasons, it is desirable that it contains the best and fullest details of the invention that are available at the time it is filed.

One reason for this is that if a provisional patent specification is inadequate, a complete or foreign patent application based on it may be declared invalid. This could happen if the invention has been used or become known after an inadequate provisional application has been filed, and before the complete or foreign application has been filed. A provisional patent application has no patent claims.

A patent application based on a provisional specification never itself becomes a granted patent. It must be followed within one year by an application including a complete specification if a granted patent is to be obtained. This period of one year can be extended by three months in respect of South Africa only.

The period of one year often proves to be inadequate and, provided the invention has not been disclosed (other than secretly) immediately after the provisional application was filed, the effective date of filing can be changed by one of two alternative means: post-dating, or re-filing.

Post-dating effectively moves the date of filing forward by any period of time up to a maximum of six months. Care must be taken that the application is not post-dated to a date later than that on which the invention was first disclosed as the new date becomes the date of filing, and the date at which patentability is assessed. Post-dating may also adversely affect rights in certain foreign countries. (See under *Obtaining patents in other countries* below.)

Re-filing means simply to file the provisional application afresh and abandon the first application. In this case the invention must not have been disclosed before the day on which the later filing is made as this then becomes the date at which patentability is assessed.

Filing a provisional application

A patent application including a provisional specification can be made by a private individual or through a patent attorney or agent. It is essential that a provisional specification be adequate. In cases where a patent application is made privately, it is highly advisable to obtain the advice of a patent attorney or agent prior to filing, or at least before the invention is disclosed.

The drafting of any patent specification is a highly specialised task. An inadequate specification can result in the loss of all rights to the invention.

Complete patent specification

A patent application which includes a complete specification is the final patent application, and it is on the complete specification that the patent will actually be granted. A complete specification may be filed in the first place if sufficient information about the invention and its implementation is available. If not, a provisional specification is more advisable.

The complete specification has more requirements than a provisional specification, and they are more stringent. One important requirement is that the complete specification must describe the best method of performing the invention known to the applicant at the time the complete specification is filed. It is thus unwise to try and hide this information – as some patent applicants try to do. The complete specification also includes the patent claims, which actually define the scope of protection which the patent will afford the patentee. A complete specification must be signed by a patent attorney or a patent agent before it can be filed at the Patent Office. The patent specification is dealt with more fully in Chapter 2.

OFFICIAL PROCEDURE

Shortly after a patent application is filed, brief details of the application are published in the *Patent Journal* by the South African Patent Office. These details include the names of the applicant and the inventor, the date of filing, and the title of the invention.

All applications are examined to ensure that they comply with the formal requirements and the applicant is advised if there are any defects in the application. No examination as to patentability is carried out by the South African Patent Office. Once all formal requirements have been fulfilled, a complete patent application is accepted, and subsequently an abridgement thereof is published in the *Patent Journal*. The 'Letters Patent' document is issued as of this date of publication but there is no guarantee that the patent is valid.

Revoking a patent

No opposition to the granting of a patent is permissible. However, any party who has grounds for objecting to the existence of the patent, for any reason, including lack of patentability, may apply for revocation of a patent. If the matter cannot be settled, it may be referred to the Court of the Commissioner of Patents for decision. This Court is a special patents court set up by the Patents Act and is presided over by a single judge of the High Court appointed on an *ad hoc* basis.

A patent may be declared *invalid* and revoked by the Court at any time during its life. This may happen on the grounds that it does not fulfill the requirements mentioned above. Usually this occurs if information comes to light which was not known at the time the patent application was filed. It can also happen if a third party successfully proves that the invention does not fulfill the requirements of novelty or inventiveness outlined above, or for a number of other technical reasons. These may include: misrepresentations made to the Patent Office in the patent application; fraud; the fact that the claims are defective; and the fact that the complete specification fails to describe the best method of performing the invention known to the patentee at the time the complete specification was filed.

AMENDMENT   Various amendments may be made to a patent or patent application if necessary. Amendments that can be made to a granted patent are subject to strict limitations. In particular, no new matter can be added to the complete specification of a granted patent. No new matter may be added to a provisional specification either.

Amendments are made to correct mistakes, or to decrease the scope of the patent in the event that it is subsequently found to be formulated too broadly. It is important to state the full reasons for making an amendment. New matter can be added only to a complete specification, and then only before acceptance by the Patent Office. Such material is added in the form of a supplementary disclosure.

HOW LONG DOES A PATENT LAST?

Under normal circumstances, in South Africa, a patent lasts for 20 years from the date on which the complete patent specification was filed at the Patent Office. However, a renewal fee must be paid annually as from the end of the third year after the complete application was filed, until the patent expires, if the patent is to be kept in force.

Each annual fee must be paid on or before the anniversary of the date of filing the complete application, subject to a six-month extension on payment of a fine. If a patent lapses because a renewal fee has not been paid, and the failure to pay the fee can be shown to have been unintentional, the patent can be restored upon application to the Registrar of Patents. A restored patent may not be enforced against persons who started to use the invention while the patent was in a state of lapse. A patent granted in terms of the former Patents Act of 1952 lasted for only 16 years from the date of filing of the complete specification. Care should be taken not to *assume* that such a patent has expired, as the law provides for an extension of term of those patents of up to five years under special circumstances. However, no extension of term is possible in terms of the present Patents Act of 1978.

ABUSE OF PATENT RIGHTS

It is interesting to note that it is the intention that patented inventions be used for the benefit of the public.

It is not therefore legal to stifle an invention for an extended period of time. If a patented invention is not used to the extent that the reasonable requirements of the public are satisfied, an interested party can, usually after three years, obtain a compulsory licence to exploit the invention. The patentee will receive a royalty which, in the absence of agreement between the parties, will be set by the Court of the Commissioner of Patents. Other forms of patent abuse can also lead to a compulsory licence being granted.

PREVENTING UNAUTHORISED USE OF AN INVENTION

Infringement – or unauthorised use of a patented invention – can be prevented through the Court of the Commissioner of Patents. In the event of others using a patented invention whilst the patent is still in force, the holder of the patent can sue, in the Court of the Commissioner of Patents, for a court order preventing them from using the invention further. A court order may also award the patent holder damages if he can establish that he has actually suffered damages. In certain circumstances a reasonable royalty may be awarded instead of damages. The Court may also order the grant of a licence.

What constitutes infringement?

As previously mentioned, the term 'use' of the invention by others in relation to infringement has a broad meaning. The Patents Act defines the effect of a patent as:

> the right to exclude other persons from making, using, exercising, disposing or offering to dispose of, or importing the invention, so that (the patentee) shall have and enjoy the whole profit and advantage accruing by reason of the invention.

Thus, contrary to popular belief, even the unauthorised private use of the invention constitutes an infringement of a patent. Also, there is no judicial limitation on the extent of what may be termed 'exercising' an invention. In order to assess whether there is infringement, it is necessary to be able to read a patent specification properly. (Chapter 2 deals with this.)

How do others know the invention is patented?

Whilst it is not compulsory to mark manufactured articles with the patent or patent application number, it is highly desirable to do so. It is also advisable to include the number in any literature, brochures, or other printed matter. This serves as a warning and deterrent to would-be infringers that a patent exists. It also has a more practical purpose in the case of infringement, in that damages may not be awarded to a patent holder if he has not adequately marked his articles of manufacture – or otherwise given notice to the public – of the fact that a granted patent exists.

An appropriate marking in South Africa is simply 'R.S.A. Pat. No...', in the case of a granted patent, and before the patent has been granted, 'R.S.A. Pat. Appl. No...'.

Nevertheless, it is always advisable to have an infringement search carried out at the South African Patent Office before embarking on the manufacture of a product similar to one available on the market. This is particularly so where costly tools, dies, jigs or other items of a capital nature are required to manufacture the product.

OBTAINING PATENTS IN OTHER COUNTRIES

Generally speaking, a patent is national and covers only one country. A South African patent thus covers only South Africa, and not Namibia or any other country. However, corresponding patents in other countries can be obtained. In some cases it is even possible to file a single patent application to cover a number of countries. A single European patent application, for example, may be filed at the European Patent Office to cover up to 18 countries, although eventually the patent will be registered nationally in each country selected (designated) by the applicant. Alternatively, individual applications can be filed in various European countries.

Individual applications must be filed in respect of countries such as the USA, Canada, Japan, Taiwan, and Australia.

The Patent Co-operation Treaty (PCT), which South Africa is poised to join in 1998, also provides a facility for temporarily securing rights in a large group of countries, before filing for the usual national or regional patent applications. The PCT, when it comes into force in South Africa, will enable a South African national to file a single patent application which can establish rights in 97 countries. It does not replace filing for the usual national or regional patent applications, but delays the necessity of doing so. It provides a facility for tailoring a patent specification according to the results of an international search; but it is a costly procedure.

South Africa is already a member of an international agreement known as the International Convention of Paris. In terms of this convention, member states have a certain period during which they can file in other member states, in spite of disclosure of an invention. In the case of patents the period is 12 months from the date on which the first application is filed in a member state.

South Africa may also join the African Regional Intellectual Property Organisation (ARIPO) at some stage in the future.

The patent laws of foreign countries vary widely and obtaining patents in foreign countries is rather complicated. It is recommended that a patent attorney or agent having knowledge of this subject should be consulted.

Filing of foreign patent applications must be considered well before one year has passed after the first patent application was filed, whether it included a provisional or a complete specification, unless the invention is still totally secret or – in the case of certain countries – fulfills other requirements.

2 How to Read a Patent Specification

As indicated in Chapter 1, the patent specification must contain a full disclosure of the invention to the public: firstly, with a view to defining what may not be done by others, without authorisation, during the life of the patent; and secondly, describing how to implement the invention after expiry of the patent. Whatever your position, if you deal in technical innovation, you will at some stage be confronted with a patent specification that you have to understand. This may be a patent specification drafted for you to cover your own invention; it may be one that you need to interpret to learn whether your product infringes it; or it may be one that reflects known technology, against which the patentability of your invention is to be measured.

When the average person reads a patent specification for the first time they often find the language pedantic and the vocabulary strange. However, once you are acquainted with the structure of a patent specification as given here, there is no reason why you should not be able to read such a document and understand its fundamental meaning.

The structure of a patent specification will vary depending on the country for which it was drafted and who drafted it, but broadly speaking all patent specifications – throughout the world – have a certain basic similarity. Very often, but not always, the various sections of the patent specification will have sub-headings the same as, or similar to, those utilised below. Basically, the specification has two parts: the *body* which is divided into various sub-sections, and the *claims*.

THE BODY OF A PATENT SPECIFICATION

The body of a patent specification generally begins with an introduction that gives the broadest outline of the field in which the invention is to be applied. This statement may also be entitled 'Field of the invention', or may take the form of an expanded title.

Background to the invention, or discussion of the prior art

Following this there may be a section that deals with the difficulties or deficiencies of known devices and the state of development of this inventive field which is generally known as the 'prior art'.

Object of the invention

There will usually then follow a paragraph entitled – or at least citing – the 'Object of the invention', although in some cases this will not be included. The object of the invention will be stated, either in extremely broad terms or in very precise terms. There may be more than one object. There are often legal reasons why the stated object varies widely, and these often depend on various national requirements of what an inventor must provide in his patent document. No great concern need be attached to the object of the invention.

Summary of the invention

Almost invariably there will follow a section that seeks to explain, in the broadest terms, what the invention is about, often under a heading that may read 'Summary of the invention'. You should not concern yourself much with this section either. It exists in the body of the specification for legal and historical reasons, and is the forerunner of the more detailed explanation of the invention. It also provides a basis for what will be recorded in the second part of the patent specification, known as the 'Claims' (dealt with under *The claims of a patent specification* below).

Detailed description of the invention

After the 'Summary of the invention', there will be a

detailed description of at least one way in which the invention can be performed or exercised. The description often refers to drawings, or includes examples. If the invention includes a physical apparatus, one particular application of the invention is generally called an 'embodiment' of the invention and is given only as one example of one way in which the invention can be expressed. If the invention includes a method or is only a method, there will often be sets of examples of how the method can be practised. These examples are given purely by way of illustration, and do not usually limit the scope of protection to which the patent holder is entitled.

Interpreting the body of a specification
It is in reading the body of the patent specification that many people new to patent specifications go wrong. This is because the body of the specification has a number of legal requirements that may seem misleading.

Firstly, the body provides a description of the 'embodiment' of the invention. This is a description of at least one way (in many countries it must be the best known way), in which the invention can be performed. This is not an advantage to the inventor, but a duty that the inventor owes to the public at large in return for the monopoly being granted to him. It is generally accepted that patents exist to provide an incentive to inventiveness and innovation, and to offer a reward for the achievement of creating an invention of a particular level of merit. In return for such a creation, the government of a country will award the inventor a monopoly in the practice of the invention for a limited period of time. On the other hand, the inventor must disclose how his invention works in such detail, and to such an extent, that after expiry of the monopoly other parties are able to implement and benefit from the invention.

It is crucial to understand that this particular description of an invention has little to do with the scope of the monopoly granted to the patentee. Often an inexperienced reader will examine the specific description of an embodiment in the patent specification, and then declare with confidence that his device is not affected by it. One simply cannot assess the monopoly that a patent affords by reading the specific description in the body of the specification. The monopoly provided by a patent is set out in the second part of a patent specification called the 'Claims'.

THE CLAIMS OF A PATENT SPECIFICATION

The claims seek to define the invention, and thus to define the monopoly that the patentee seeks to secure as a proprietary right.

The first claim is normally the broadest in scope, and aims to define the invention in the widest possible terms in order to claim the largest area of technology for the inventor. This is why the language used in the claims may seem vague or indeterminate. The patent attorney or agent has the task of framing a definition of the invention that has a wide meaning, but is nonetheless anything but vague or uncertain. Vagueness or uncertainty in the language of a claim is a good ground for invalidity of the patent.

Ideally, a patent claim, in particular the broadest claim, should claim everything that is new and which the patentee wishes to protect, but must exclude everything that has been done before or has been previously described in the literature.

A claim consists of various listed parts, which form an *apparatus* being claimed; or details of various actions or operations, set out for the performance of a *method* being claimed. These parts or operations are referred to as the 'integers' of a claim. Some of the integers may be described in a purely physical way, for example: 'a rectangular block of steel'. The integer may, however, be described in a more functional manner, for example: 'a metallic body shaped to be located in a stable manner on a planar surface on any one side of pairs of opposing sides'. A brief reflection on these two definitions will show that they are not equal in meaning. Although the resultant effect of the more functional definition may apparently be the same as that of the simple description of the body as a rectangular block, an octahedral cross-sectioned block will fall within the scope of the latter, but not of the former.

The broadest claim of a patent must thus include at least one new feature or integer, or a new combination of features or integers.

The claims section comprises a series of numbered sentences. Even though some of the claims may be more than one page long, they remain single sentences and, accordingly, not a single full stop will be present in the whole of the text of any one claim.

Interpreting the claims of a specification

The basic rules for interpreting the claims of a patent are simple. In fact, the rules are so simple that in many cases people struggle with them. It is in applying the rules that difficulties may arise, and it is in this area that the expertise of the patent attorney or agent is appropriate.

The rules of interpretation of a claim are based on the principle that the scope of the monopoly is defined in the claims. Thus if an invention was previously known to the public it cannot be patented because it is not new: it is 'anticipated' by a prior device or publication. However, if an invention is made public or produced after the effective date of an existing patent, and complies with the definition of the patented invention in the claims, it will infringe the patent if made by an unauthorised third party.

To express the principle in another way: if a device or description of it existed before the effective date of a patent that contains a claim covering the device, that claim is anticipated and the patent is invalid. If the device is made available by an unauthorised person after the effective date of the patent, and complies with the definition of the invention in a claim, it infringes the patent.

Does it infringe?

How does one test whether an invention complies with the definition set out in a claim, and therefore infringes it? Here are the rules:

• If all the integers, as set out in a claim, are present in the device, then that device falls squarely within the definition of the claim and it infringes the patent.

- However, if a device has fewer integers than those set out in the claim – in all but exceptional circumstances – it does not infringe the claim.
- If the device has all of the integers of a claim and one or more others as well, it nonetheless still complies with the definition since it has, as a minimum, those integers set out in the claim. It thus infringes the patent.

SUMMARY

If a device or a disclosure is made available to the public prior to the date of a patent but has fewer integers than set out in the claim, it will not anticipate the patent. By the same token if the same device was made available to the public after the date of the patent, it will not infringe the patent, since it does not comply with the definition of the patent in that at least one integer of the claims will be missing.

As a rule of thumb, if a product can be made with even one integer fewer than is set out in the patent claim, it will not infringe the patent. There are some theories of claim interpretation that require examination of whether the integer being left out is an essential one or not, and various other doctrines that can be considered, such as an obvious mechanical equivalent of an integer, and a patent attorney or agent should be consulted regarding those.

It will be apparent that when drafting a claim to an invention, it is desirable to include the barest minimum of integers that will describe the invention, while excluding what is old, in order to obtain the widest scope of protection. The art of drawing such a claim is therefore not a simple one and should not be attempted by anyone not adequately skilled.

3 Know-how

Know-how is a rather strange concept, and not easy to define. In general terms, we can say that know-how is a body of knowledge, developed or collected in relation to the carrying out of a process, or the conduct of a particular business, and that is not available to others involved in the same or a similar business. It is usually unpatentable in itself, although it may relate to ways in which a patented invention, for example, can best or most effectively be implemented. It may relate to methods of conducting business, culinary recipes, computer programs, or simply to a collection of information. It is usually regarded as encompassing trade secrets, unpatentable commercial techniques such as marketing schemes, unpublished operating instructions, teaching manuals, plans, blueprints, formulae for whatever purpose, and many other items. In summary, know-how may assume the form of any body of information that is proprietary to its owner, and that may be used to achieve a commercial result, usually with advantage.

SELLING OR LICENSING KNOW-HOW

Know-how, for the purposes of sale or licensing, is very much like any other form of intellectual property. However, because of its nature, it must be treated with substantial care. The reason for this is that its very existence depends on the fact that in order to be of any value, it must be kept secret. The instant it falls into the public domain (that is, loses its secrecy) it becomes worthless to the original holder, as every one of his competitors can then avail themselves of it and the original advantage is lost.

Because of this characteristic of know-how, the form of remuneration agreed to by a holder of know-how who is licensing another person under that know-how, may be different from the form it would have taken if a registered right been involved. (See Chapter 13 for types of remuneration usually payable in terms of licence agreements.) When licensing know-how – because of the danger of the know-how losing its secrecy – the tendency is often to require a rather greater initial, non-refundable, lump-sum payment, in addition to a running royalty, commission or other fee, proportional to the extent that the licensee uses the know-how. Once know-how loses its confidentiality and becomes part of the public domain, it would be unfair, if not illegal, to require the licensee to continue to pay royalties or other fees.

DRAFTING THE KNOW-HOW AGREEMENT

It must, however, be remembered that if the know-how falls into the public domain owing to fault on the part of the licensee, or another person under a confidentiality obligation, a claim for damages can be pursued against the discloser.

This makes it important to draft secrecy undertakings in know-how agreements with great care. It is also necessary to take care in transferring the know-how to the licensee. It is an advantage if the transfer takes place in two stages: first, an initial transfer, simply to show that the know-how does exist, accompanied by payment of the non-refundable lump sum by the licensee to the owner of the know-how; and secondly, the transfer of the balance of the know-how to the licensee. It is to be noted that a substantial lump sum payment ensures that the licensee has a proprietary interest in maintaining the confidentiality of the know-how. On the other hand the licensee is entitled to require certain guarantees that the know-how will give certain results, particularly where the know-how owner claims particular technical results that the know-how is purported to achieve.

One substantial advantage of the secret nature of know-how is the fact that it does not automatically fall into the public domain, unlike a patent or registered design when it expires. It can theoretically remain secret forever, and therefore indefinitely be an advantage to its owner and any licensees.

EXPIRY OF THE KNOW-HOW LICENCE

There is another consideration that should be dealt with in a know-how agreement. This is whether or not the licensee is entitled to continue using the know-how when the licence expires, or is cancelled for any reason. Careful consideration must be given to this, as provisions agreed upon would usually be different according to the reason for which the licence was cancelled, and the intention of the parties if the licence expires within a given time. Often the attitude is that once a know-how agreement has run its full term the licensee has 'purchased' the right to continue using the know-how. On the other hand, the know-how may be considered to last forever, and the licensee has only 'leased' it – at least until it loses its secrecy. In this view, there is no right to continued use of the know-how. It is thus important for the two parties to agree on this aspect at the outset and to deal with it in the licence contract. In the case of know-how necessary to exploit a patent, the former is probably the more correct as the licensee would be entitled to continued and free use of the subject matter of the patent after its expiry in terms of the Patent Law.

Accordingly, whilst know-how can be treated similarly to other intellectual property, special caution in its licensing is required.

4 Trade Marks

A trade mark is essentially a means of identifying a product, whether goods or services. It is often a brand name but it can be any sign capable of being represented graphically, including a picture, signature, colour, numeral, shape, configuration, pattern or a container for goods, or any combination of these.

Trade marks are protected by common law and by statute. Common law protection is restricted, and getting an effective remedy can be onerous and expensive. Trade mark registrations, by contrast, provide wide ranging protection and powerful remedies against infringement. The relevant legislation is the Trade Marks Act No.194 of 1993, although the former law, namely the Trade Marks Act No.62 of 1963, continues to apply in some respects to trade marks applied for, or registered in terms of that Act.

The Trade Marks Act defines the function of a trade mark as distinguishing one person's goods (or services) from those of another. It follows that trade marks are registered for certain goods or categories of goods or services.

WHAT CANNOT BE REGISTERED AS A TRADE MARK?

In terms of the Trade Marks Act, the following may not be registered:

- a mark that does not conform with the definition of a trade mark;

- a mark that is not capable of distinguishing the relevant goods or services, or that is a descriptive term for them,

or that has become customary or commonplace as regards the goods or services;

- any mark where the applicant has no *bona fide* claim to proprietorship;

- any mark where there is no *bona fide* intention to use the mark;

- a mark that consists of the shape, configuration or colour of goods where such features are necessary to obtain a specific technical result or are dictated by the nature of the product;

- a mark that is essentially a reproduction or imitation of a well-known trade mark entitled to protection under the International Convention of Paris for the same or similar goods;

- a mark where the application for registration is *mala fide*, or in bad faith;

- a coat of arms, seal or flag of the Republic, or of other countries;

- any word, letter or device indicating state patronage;

- a mark that contains matter declared by regulation as being prohibited;

- a container for goods, or the shape, configuration, colour or pattern of goods, where such registration will be likely to limit the development of any art or industry;

- matter that is inherently deceptive or would be likely to deceive or cause confusion or would be otherwise against the law or morality or would give offence;

- a mark that, as a result of the manner in which it has

been used, would be likely to cause deception or confusion;

• any mark that is similar to a trade mark already applied for, registered, or in use; and

• any mark that would take unfair advantage of a registered and well known trade mark or that would be likely to cause deception or confusion with a registered or unregistered well known trade mark.

These are the broad legal principles and practical guidelines. In certain instances one can register a trade mark that ostensibly offends against these principles, but it is advisable to take them into consideration wherever possible. Furthermore, at the time of selection of a trade mark, its meaning in other languages should be considered to avoid possible negative connotations, or even embarrassment. Whilst there is an understandable enthusiasm to use descriptive terms for trade marks or brand names, this is not advisable. Although commercially appealing, descriptive trade marks are neither always legally acceptable nor beneficial in the long term.

The more descriptive a particular term, the more it is likely to be used by other traders, as they might also wish to describe their products in the same terms. Use of a word that is commonly required by other traders is to be avoided as the idea behind using a trade mark is to distinguish one's own products from those of others. It is noteworthy that, in order for a trade mark to be registrable, the Trade Marks Act requires that the trade mark be 'capable of distinguishing' the trade marked goods or services from those of other traders.

A trade mark is usually used in combination with descriptive words and the two should not be confused. It is the trade mark that is the exclusive property of its owner, whereas the descriptive words should be available for use by competitors. Whatever else it may be, a trade mark should be appealing and have an agreeable image or connotation.

BRANDS AND BRANDING IN THE TRADE MARK CONTEXT

Goods have been branded for many centuries. Initially brands indicated proprietorship but today they serve a very different purpose. By general definition, a brand is a particular make of goods or an identifying trade mark or label. In business terms, the word 'brand' refers to much more than this. While it is possible to have a trade mark without a brand it is inconceivable that there can be a brand without a trade mark. However, although a trade mark is invariably the basis of any brand, 'brand' encompasses more than the trade mark associated with it. Like trade marks, brands serve to distinguish or identify but they also promise quality, and certain features and associations – some of which we could only define as a certain 'feel'.

In a short hand way, the brand represents to the purchaser every thing the marketer has put behind the product. It is perhaps from this that the value of brands and branding arises. At the moment when the purchase is made the brand represents every effort that has been put into the creation, manufacture and marketing of the product. It is the final link between the product and the purchaser. The difference between a brand and a commodity can be summed up in the phrase 'added value', as the brand embodies for the user additional attributes that, while they may be considered to be intangible, are still very real.

In today's marketing environments, brands have become immensely powerful marketing tools. From the consumer point of view brands serve primarily as a sign of identification but they also serve as a guarantee of consistent quality. From the marketing point of view brands can, in addition to identifying, serve as a means of self expression for the consumer.

The value of a brand name can thus be immense and businesses that have brand names have been sold for many times the value of their tangible assets. Because the foundation of every brand is the trade mark, the brand also provides the owner of the brand with exclusive rights to the use of the trade mark and to legal protection of those rights.

PROTECTION OF WELL-KNOWN MARKS

South Africa became a signatory to the Paris Convention on 1 December 1947. Under this convention signatories must provide protection for marks considered to be well known in the contracting country. South Africa did not initially pass legislation to incorporate its obligations under the Paris Convention into its National Laws. The position was rectified in Section 35 of the present Act, which provides for protection of a trade mark that is well known in South Africa, whether or not the owner of the trade mark carries on business, or has any goodwill in South Africa. A well-known trade mark is thus protected if the owner is:

• a national of a convention country; or

• domiciled in, or has a real and effective industrial or commercial establishment in, a convention country.

In terms of the Trade Marks Act, the owner of a trade mark must be able to show that a trade mark has a reputation in South Africa. The Act states that due regard must be given to knowledge of the trade mark in the relevant sector of the public, as well as to knowledge that exists as a result of promotion of the trade mark. This kind of knowledge may be acquired through spill-over advertising, for example; or through South Africans travelling abroad and so being exposed to the trade mark.

Two factors now make real protection available to well-known trade marks in South Africa. First, an amendment to Section 35 of the Trade Marks Act has clarified how to determine whether a trade mark is well-known in South Africa. Secondly, in the recent MacDonald's case, the appeal court decided that for a trade mark to be considered well-known, a 'substantial number' of people should know the mark. (The degree of knowledge required is similar to that of the existing law of passing-off.)

WHAT SHOULD BE DONE BEFORE USING A NEW TRADE MARK?

Prior to adopting a trade mark, it is advisable to determine whether the trade mark (or trading name) will infringe any registered or unregistered trade marks that already exist. Existing registered trade marks or pending applications can be discovered by conducting a search through the Trade Marks Register for marks that may be confusingly similar to the one selected – whether visually, phonetically, or conceptually. This 'searching' procedure is not only important, but is also fairly complicated and usually requires the attention of a specialist.

Such searches can determine only whether the proposed mark conflicts with existing registered or pending trade marks. With regard to unregistered trade marks already in use, it is often extremely difficult to obtain knowledge of such marks unless an intimate knowledge of the particular trade exists. In doubtful cases it may be advisable to conduct a survey of the relevant trade.

The importance of checking on the availability for use of a trade mark cannot be overstressed. If you begin to use a trade mark and are subsequently prevented by a third party who has rights to the trade mark, enormous costs may be wasted – for example in the preparation and production of stationery, brochures, advertising materials, packaging and products bearing the mark. Also, any goodwill or repute developed in the mark will be wasted and may even benefit the entitled party. In any event, it would be best to consult a trade mark attorney or agent before commencing use of a trade mark.

WHY REGISTER A TRADE MARK?

It is not compulsory to register a trade mark before it is used. The common law of South Africa offers some protection, but only where trade marks have been used and have acquired a reputation and goodwill in South Africa. On the other hand, there are some real advantages to be obtained by registering a trade mark:

- The prevention of infringement of a trade mark is easier, less time-consuming and less costly in cases where a registered trade mark is held, as opposed to proceedings based on common law rights.

- In the event of infringement, damages may be claimed from the infringer.

- The acquisition of rights through registration is generally much quicker than building up the required common law repute, and goodwill, through use.

- Registration allows for the effective appointment and control of licensees and franchisees.

- Registered trade marks are relatively easy to assign to third parties.

- Registered trade marks may be used as security for loans.

- A South African trade mark registration can be of assistance in obtaining registered trade mark protection in other countries.

WHO MAY APPLY TO REGISTER A TRADE MARK?

Generally, only the person or company who can claim to be the owner of a trade mark and who intends to use it, or is using it, may validly seek its registration. However, the applicant need not intend to use the trade mark himself if he is the trustee of a company about to be formed, and that company will become the owner of the trade mark; or if a licensee will be appointed and the licensee will use the trade mark.

THE REGISTRATION PROCEDURE

An application to register a trade mark is made by filing details of the proprietor, the trade mark, and the goods or services in respect of which it will be used, together with the necessary forms and revenue stamps, at the Trade Marks Office. It is sometimes necessary to apply to register a trade mark in more than one 'class', as a separate application is necessary for each 'class' in which protection is desired. Each class in the trade marks register relates to a general type of product or service.

For example, explosives and fireworks fall into class 13, whilst jewellery falls into class 14, and leather goods into class 18. Some classes relate essentially to the materials from which products are made and because of this certain products can fall into more than one class. Thus you should take care when deciding in which classes you should register a trade mark.

In addition, a definition of the goods or services has to be included with each trade mark application. It is important to define the goods or services correctly and in sufficient breadth, as this definition will to a large extent determine the right to restrain others from using or registering the same – or a similar – trade mark, in the same class, but possibly in respect of different goods.

Some months after filing, the Registrar will begin his examination of the application, both from formal and substantive points of view. It is at this stage that he may raise objections based on exclusions provided in the Trade Marks Act (see *What cannot be registered as a trade mark?* above) or on an earlier existing registration or application. He may require certain endorsements to be entered against the application. These often have the effect of limiting the goods in respect of which the trade mark is to be registered. Alternatively they may make it clear that registration of the trade mark does not provide the owner with exclusivity in respect of certain parts or words contained in the mark. An application to register a trade mark, for example, 'good 'n clean 'n fresh' would beg the endorsement that registration of the trade mark would not preclude others from using the words 'good', 'clean' or 'fresh' separately and apart from the trade mark. These objections may lead to debate and possibly a hearing with the Registrar. In due course – and after any objections of the Registrar have been overcome – he will issue acceptance of the application.

The application is then advertised in the monthly *Patent Journal*. After this, third parties may oppose the application (see below). After the opposition stage, unless any opposing third party is successful in its objection, the registration certificate will be issued. It can take two years or longer to obtain registration. For this reason it is important that a search is conducted before you begin using the trade mark. The results of the search will show whether you can do so, and the trade mark can then be used while awaiting registration.

HOW CAN THE APPLICATION FOR REGISTRATION BE OPPOSED?

Within a period of three months from the date of advertisement in the *Patent Journal*, any interested party may lodge opposition to the registration of the trade mark. Extensions of this period can be obtained on application to the Registrar.

Various grounds of opposition are available and include conflict with prior registered or common law trade marks. Generally trade marks that do not conform to the requirements for registration may be opposed.

Opposition is an important facility, especially in that it affords trade mark owners the opportunity of ensuring that competitors do not register similar trade marks.

HOW LONG DOES A TRADE MARK REGISTRATION LAST?

A trade mark registration lasts for ten years as from the date of filing the application for its registration and may be renewed indefinitely for subsequent periods of ten years at a time.

CAN A TRADE MARK REGISTRATION BE CANCELLED?

You can apply for cancellation of a trade mark that has already been registered on the basis that you are the true proprietor of the trade mark; or that the trade mark has been wrongly registered, being non-distinctive or in conflict with an existing mark; or that the registration is contrary to the law.

Registration of a trade mark is made on the basis that it is intended to be used. A third party who is inhibited by the registration can apply for cancellation of the trade mark registration. A continuous period of non-use of five years or more can form the basis for such cancellation proceedings. In addition, the owner of a trade mark should not allow it to be used deceptively or in conflict with the undertakings of any endorsements it may bear, as this can also afford grounds for cancellation of the registration.

HOW SHOULD A TRADE MARK BE USED?

Everyday words such as gramophone, aspirin, linoleum and escalator were once valuable trade marks. However, they were not used correctly as trade marks and became the accepted English words describing these articles. In this way, they failed to distinguish articles made by one person from similar articles made by someone else. Proprietary rights to such trade marks may be forfeited in such circumstances. The general aim, therefore, is to use the trade mark in such a manner as to maintain its distinctiveness. Keeping to the following guidelines should ensure the continued validity of a trade mark:

- Use the trade mark as an adjective – never as a proper noun or verb:
  'I always use JAXX® flea powder on my dogs' – correct!
  'I always jaxx my dogs' – wrong!

- Never add an apostrophe -'s' to the trade mark:
  'I endorse JAXX® flea powder's ability to eradicate fleas' – correct!
  'I endorse Jaxx's ability to eradicate fleas' – wrong!

- Use the trade mark in a way that distinguishes it from other common words or its context – for instance, use capital letters in text.

- Although not compulsory, it is advisable always to indicate that the word is a trade mark. This can be done in a number of ways. The most common is to print the words 'Trade Mark', or the abbreviation, 'TM'. Once it is actually registered, the internationally recognised symbol ® should be placed in close proximity to the trade mark wherever it is used. It is, however, a criminal offence to indicate that a trade mark is registered when this is not so, even if it is the subject of a trade mark application but is not yet actually registered.

Infringement
The usual kind of infringement is where a third party

uses a trade mark that is identical or confusingly similar to the one registered, and the goods are so similar that there is a likelihood either of confusion or deception. This is termed statutory infringement, and can be stopped by application proceedings in the High Court or before the Registrar of Trade Marks.

LICENSING: HOW TO PROTECT LICENSOR AND LICENSEE

As a registered proprietor of a trade mark, you are obviously entitled to use your own mark. You can also authorise third parties to use it. In such cases it is sometimes to your advantage to register your licensees on the *Trade Marks Register* as 'registered users'.

DOES A REGISTRATION COVER OTHER COUNTRIES?

A South African trade mark registration covers only the Republic of South Africa. It does not afford protection in any of South Africa's neighbouring states, or any other country. A separate application for registration must be filed in each of these countries if protection is required. Applications for registration in foreign countries can be based on a South African trade mark application. 'Convention priority' may be claimed if foreign applications are filed within six months after filing of the South African application. Such applications are made in terms of the International Convention of Paris, as in the case of patents, but the period in which you can claim 'Convention priority' is limited to six months.

5 The Protection of Trading Names

Protecting trade *marks* is important. Of similar importance is the parallel role of business *names*. While it is true that consumers identify products mostly through their associated trade marks or brand names, it is often overlooked that many consumers first become aware of the existence of a product because they already know about the business that manufactures it. It follows from this that the name by which a business is known to the public can be of vital importance to the successful marketing of a product, as it often carries with it a tacit or expressed guarantee of the quality – or standards of service – that have become synonymous with the name of the business.

It is therefore of great importance to a business to be able to protect the valuable asset of its trading name against unauthorised use or unlawful passing-off, as well as protecting trade marks used for marketing its products.

Apart from every trader's common law right to prevent unauthorised parties from 'muscling-in' on the goodwill that attaches to the trader's trading name and logo (if any), there are several sets of statutory enactments that reinforce this position. If used carefully – either separately or in combination – these laws can afford a trader practically complete protection of his trading name. Contraventions of these Acts can actually be subject to criminal as well as civil sanctions.

A trader can usually protect his current or future trading name, or prevent third parties from registering an important brand or product name as a trading name, by applying for registration of the name as a trade mark.

Alternatively, he can apply to register it as a company or close corporation name, and – in addition, or instead – as a defensive company name.

METHODS OF PROTECTING A TRADING NAME

The company name

If a trader wants to use a company or a close corporation as his trading vehicle, the name under which he registers it will itself have sufficient individuality to ensure that it cannot be readily confused, in the mind of the public, with another similar entity. This is done in terms of the Companies Act or the Close Corporation Act. In time, the registered name should attract goodwill and individual identity as far as the relevant consumers are concerned.

'Defensive' registration

Sometimes, for various reasons, a company or close corporation either ceases to exist or changes its name; or it decides to trade under the name of its product instead of under its own registered name; or the name of the product, rather than the name of its proprietor, becomes the basis of identification as far as the public is concerned. Under such circumstances, the trader may register the trading name or product name 'defensively' for periods of two years at a time. Under a defensive registration the applicant secures the use of the appropriate word (name, or combination of words), for his exclusive use as far as the company or close corporation register is concerned. He is then entitled to defend that exclusive use against outside interference. The exclusivity granted by a defensive registration exists irrespective of whether or not a third party wishes to use the name in conjunction with a business of a totally different nature.

As regards objections to a defensive registration, the Companies Act lays down a comprehensive procedure. This applies to registering and extending the registration of a defensive name, and also to an objection to the registration of the name by a party who regards his own rights to that word, or combination of words, as being infringed by such registration. Under the Companies Act, the Registrar of Companies can make and enforce any order on a person to change a defensive name or the registered name of a company or a close corporation.

Other legal remedies

On the other hand, if the holder of a registered company or defensive name finds that another company or close corporation – or even a private person – is trading under the same name in an unregistered form, he cannot appeal to the sanctions provided by the Companies or Close Corporation Acts. What he can do is to invoke the provisions of the Business Names Act, 1960.

There are also remedies under the Trade Marks Act if the name is registered as a trade mark, and thus it is advisable (even if the trading name is registered under the Companies or Close Corporations Acts), to have concurrent protection for the name under the Trade Marks Act (see Chapter 3).

Protection on the Internet

Consideration should also be given to registering a name as a domain name for the purposes of the Internet (see Chapter 10).

HOW TO INVOKE PROTECTION

Under the Companies and Close Corporation Acts

The procedure for invoking the protection of the Companies and Close Corporation Acts is to send a letter of objection to the Registrar with payment of his objection fee in revenue stamps. On receiving the objection, the Registrar notifies the other party of the nature and scope of the objection and invites his response. He then relays this response to the objector, and the matter is dealt with by way of alternating invitations to the two parties to state their conflicting views on the matter, after which the Registrar either dismisses the objection or orders the party against whom it was taken to change the name in question.

This decision is subject to review by the High Court. In legal terms, in this case, the term 'review' does not carry the usual onus – of showing that the Registrar had not applied his mind to the matter. It is, in fact, merely a form of appeal to the High Court against the Registrar's decision.

Once the 'review' procedure has been exhausted, the order made must, if it consists of a directive to change a name, be complied with within the time laid down in the order. Failure to comply constitutes an offence that is punishable in terms of Section 44(1)(b) of the Act, by a fine of R40.00 per day of the period during which the failure continues.

Under the Business Names Act

If, however, the name that forms the subject of the complaint is not registered under the Companies Act as a company or close corporation, or as a defensive name, the procedure is to invoke the protection of Section 5 of the Business Names Act, which is also administered by the Registrar of Companies. Such an objection is also initiated by a letter of objection and the procedure is similar to – but not quite as lengthy as – that prescribed by the Companies or Close Corporations Acts. It results, eventually, in an order that can also be reviewed by the High Court, and that carries, on non-compliance, the sanction of a fine of R10.00 per day of the period during which the non-compliance continues.

To sum up, the goodwill attaching to a proprietor's registered trade marks, as well as his registered and unregistered trading names, is capable of comprehensive protection. It is advisable to make the fullest use possible of protection mechanisms as soon as your business or products begin to acquire a valuable identity among consumers.

6 Registered Designs

The registration of designs is governed by the Designs Act of 1993. Designs registered in terms of the previous Designs Act of 1967 are still governed by that Act. Unlike most other countries, in South Africa the current Designs Act provides for two different types of design registrations, namely, aesthetic designs and functional designs. The former Act provided for aesthetic designs only.

WHAT IS A REGISTERED DESIGN?

A registered design is a monopoly granted by the State to the proprietor of a design for a specific period of time in exchange for disclosure of the design to the public for their use, after expiry of the period for which the registration is granted.

A registered design relates to the shape or appearance of an article, whether or not it is patentable. Thus an application to register a design is based on drawings, photographs, or other pictures, which clearly illustrate the shape or appearance of the relevant article.

A registered design is property and may be sold (generally by way of assignment) or licensed for use by others (generally effected by way of a licence contract).

WHAT CAN BE REGISTERED AS A DESIGN?

Aesthetic designs

Aesthetic designs are granted exclusively for the aesthetic appearance of an article and are judged solely by the eye, for example: an article of jewellery; the shape of a drinking glass; the pattern applied to a fabric. This type of design does not include articles whose shape is dictated solely by their function. To qualify as an

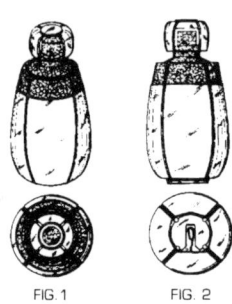

FIG. 1   FIG. 2

Design of a container for Yves St Laurent

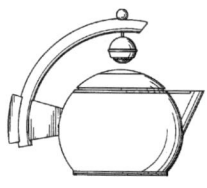

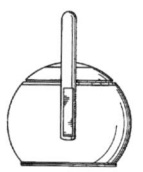

Kettle design of AMC International (Alfa Metalcraft Corporation AG)

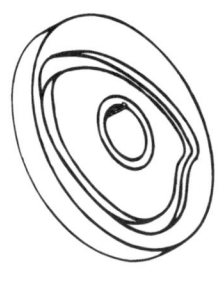

Cam plate for indexing mechanism

aesthetic design there must be at least some aesthetic component inherent in the article. The terms usually used to convey this component of the article are: shape, configuration, pattern or ornamentation.

Functional designs

Functional designs, on the other hand, do not require that the article has any aesthetic appeal. An article whose shape is dictated, at least to a certain extent, by its function can be protected as a functional design. Articles that qualify as functional designs include, for example, the mechanism of a clutch pencil, mouldings, and the like. It should be noted, however, that many functional designs do have an element of aesthetic appeal which has been introduced by the designer. Such designs can also be registered as aesthetic designs insofar as they relate to aesthetic appearance, and should therefore be considered as both aesthetic and functional designs.

The Designs Act further specifically provides that an integrated circuit topography, a mask work and series of mask works can also be registered as functional designs. This provides effective protection for semi-conductor chips or integrated circuits.

As far as *spare parts* are concerned, the Designs Act does not categorically deny protection to a spare part as a functional design. The Act does, however, provide that:

> no feature of pattern, shape or configuration of an article in the nature of a spare part is afforded any rights as a functional design.

Exactly what is meant by this provision is unclear. A 'spare part' is also not defined in the Act. The provisions regarding spare parts will have to be clarified by amendment or by the Courts. The general understanding of the Act in its present form is that it is not possible to obtain effective protection for spare parts as *functional* designs, although there appears to be nothing to stop the registration of such designs, for what it is worth. There is further no prohibition against the registration of an aesthetic design for a spare part where the spare part has *aesthetic* features. In many cases, spare parts have functional features only and very little in the way of aesthetic features; but exceptions will most certainly exist. Certain body parts of motor vehicles would be an example.

WHAT ARE THE REQUIREMENTS FOR REGISTRATION?

Any aesthetic design which is 'new or original' at the date of application for its registration, can be registered. A functional design is required to be 'new and not commonplace in the art in question'. A design, aesthetic or functional, is 'new' if:

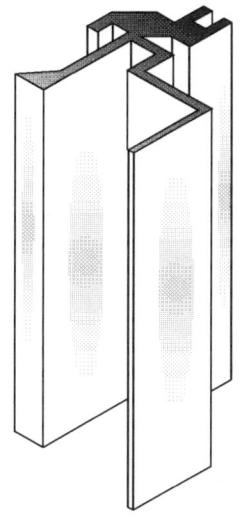

Functional design: extruded aluminium structural section

- it does not form part of the 'state of the art' immediately before the date of application for its registration. The state of the art includes all matter that has been made available to the public (whether in South Africa or elsewhere) by written description, by use, or in any other way, and it also includes matter contained in design applications already filed; or

- it does not form part of the state of the art on the 'release date' (if this is the earlier date). The release date is the date on which the design was first made available to the public by the proprietor of the design.

The Designs Act provides that a design application may be filed within six months of the release date of the article embodying the design. This means that an article can be sold for up to six months before a design application has to be filed. However, if a third party started using a design after the release date of the article embodying the design, and before application is made for a registered design, he may continue to use the design after a design has been registered. It is therefore preferable to apply for registration of a design before releasing it to the public.

WHO MAY APPLY TO REGISTER A DESIGN?

A registered design may be applied for by the proprietor (owner) of the design. The author or creator of the design is automatically the owner of the design and entitled to register it unless the design was made for another party (including a company). In this case, that other party is the owner and entitled to register the design. Usually a design is considered to have been made for some other person if the author or creator has been paid in one way or another to make the design. Whilst the applicant for a registered design must be the owner (proprietor) of the design, proof of ownership is not required. Proof may, however, be needed if the registered design becomes the subject of litigation.

MAKING A REGISTERED DESIGN APPLICATION

An application for registration of a design is made by filing representations of the design together with the necessary forms and revenue stamps at the Designs Office in Pretoria. The representations may be in the form of drawings or other pictures, illustrating the relevant article in sufficient detail to show clearly the new and original features of the design. Although photographs may be used, they are not favoured by the Designs Office owing to procedural difficulties that they cause, but they may be used where other pictures cannot be practically produced.

In terms of the Designs Act, aesthetic designs are registered in part 'A' of the Designs Register; functional designs in part 'F'. It is possible to register a design for an article in both part A and part F, and also to change a part A application to a part F application and vice versa.

HOW LONG DOES A REGISTERED DESIGN LAST?

A registered aesthetic design remains in force for a maximum of 15 years, whilst a registered functional design remains in force for a maximum of 10 years. In each case annual renewal fees must be paid as from the end of the third year from the date of registration or the release date (whichever is earlier), in order to keep the design in force. In the case of designs registered under the former Designs Act, renewal fees are payable annually after the first or second five-yearly renewal fee falls due subsequent to 1 May 1995.

A registered design may be declared invalid by the High Court at any time during its life on the basis that it did not fulfill the requirements for registration at the time the application for registration was made.

HOW MAY A REGISTERED DESIGN BE ENFORCED?

A registered design, aesthetic or functional, entitles the owner to sue someone who makes unauthorised use of the design, for an interdict preventing such person from further using the design. Such a Court order may also award the design owner damages in the event that they exist. The unauthorised use of a registered design is termed infringement. Infringement of a registered design may also be claimed where an offending design is not necessarily identical to that of the proprietor, but is 'not substantially different' from the registered design.

In infringement litigation in connection with *aesthetic* designs, the comparison between the alleged infringing article and the registered design has, under the former law, been based on a visual test. Whilst there have not yet been judicial decisions under the present law, it is expected that such a visual test will be applied to both aesthetic and functional designs. A visual test may, of course, prove to be inappropriate in some cases of functional designs, such as in the case of integrated circuit topography and mask works. Further, a determination of whether an article is the same as, or not substantially different from, a registered design, is influenced by the degree of similarity between the registered design, and designs available before the date of application of the registered design (or the release date). It remains to be seen whether functional designs will be dealt with in quite the same way as aesthetic designs, as there are no Court decisions regarding functional designs as yet. In many instances the threat of legal action may be sufficient to stop the infringement.

ABUSE OF REGISTERED DESIGN RIGHTS

As with patents, registered designs are supposed to be used for the benefit of the public. Thus, if a registered design is not used to the extent that the reasonable requirements of the public are satisfied, an interested party can obtain a compulsory licence to make articles embodying the registered design. He pays a royalty to the design holder, which, in the absence of agreement between the parties, is set by the High Court. Other forms of registered design abuse can also lead to granting of a compulsory licence.

HOW DO OTHERS KNOW THE DESIGN IS REGISTERED?

It is common practice to mark articles manufactured according to a registered design with a reference to that design. Such reference would take the form of 'RSA Registered Design No ...' where the number is the number allocated by the Designs Office.

Marking is not, however, compulsory. Where an article is not marked, a search can be done at the Registered Designs Office in Pretoria to find out whether a registered design exists. Failure to mark articles properly may prejudice the owner of a registered design if damages are to be claimed.

OBTAINING REGISTERED DESIGNS IN OTHER COUNTRIES

A registered design, generally speaking, covers only one country (for example South Africa), but corresponding registered designs can be obtained in other countries. Where a design has been registered or used publicly, application for registration in foreign countries must be made within six months from the date of filing the application in the first country. Such applications are governed by the International Convention of Paris, in the same way as patents and trade marks. Public use within the grace period created by the release date concept may negate these rights. This is another reason to apply for registration of a design before releasing it to the public.

Golf club heads, design of Callaway Golf Co

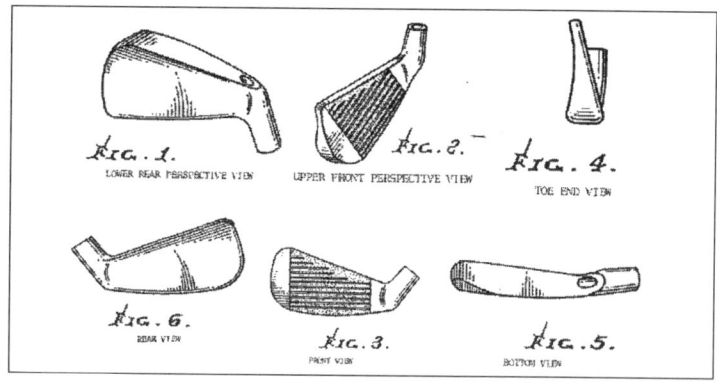

7 Unlawful Competition and Restraints of Trade

UNLAWFUL COMPETITION

In South African law there is a broad category of conduct that is generally described as 'unlawful competition'. Unlawful competition is not limited to any specific kind of unlawful action and is not covered by legislation. It is a body of common law that has been developed by the Courts basically interpreting the ancient Roman Law that has been incorporated into South Africa's legal system. It falls under the branch of law known as 'delict'.

Unlawful competition means that any person has the right to stop a third party from conducting business or other activities in a manner that prejudices such person in the conduct of his own business or activities. This right exists whether or not there are patents, registered designs, trade marks, or copyright in force; but the activities of the third party must be unlawful in some way.

In commerce, free trade and competition are fundamental. However, certain types of conduct go beyond the bounds of free trade and competition, usually with the intention of gaining an advantage over a competitor in an unfair or unlawful manner. The Courts apply general principles of the law of delict to such conduct, and may declare it unlawful, grant an order preventing such conduct, and award damages to the aggrieved party.

There are certain developed and well defined categories of conduct amounting to unlawful competition. In those cases the requirements are well established. Besides these, our Courts have now accepted that fairness and the general sense of justice of the community are the standards of measurement for actions falling outside the well established categories. Not all conduct that may be considered unfair will necessarily be unlawful. The Courts must decide in each case whether what has been done amounts to unlawful competition; but in general, in order for conduct to constitute unlawful competition, three basic elements must be present:

- the act must be unlawful in one way or another;
- there must be actual damage or the likelihood of damage to the person affected by the unlawful conduct; and
- the conduct must interfere with a right or legal entitlement of the person affected.

SOME ESTABLISHED CATEGORIES OF UNLAWFUL COMPETITION

Passing-off

This is a misrepresentation by one person that his goods or services are those of another person. This is the best developed form of unlawful competition in South Africa. The misrepresentation may arise through the use of a trade mark or get-up (general appearance, packaging, manner of presentation, etc.) that are identical or confusingly similar to those of someone else; or as a consequence of some other misrepresentation, including false impressions created by advertising campaigns and the like.

Copy at right infringes both the trade mark and common law rights of Luster Products (inc)

The wronged party must have a reputation and goodwill in its own trade mark or get-up as a consequence of extensive use, and the repute must exist in South Africa. Even very extensive use elsewhere in the world will not suffice if it cannot be shown that there is no repute and goodwill in South Africa. The existence or otherwise of a reputation is a question of fact: it may be possible for a sufficient repute to have been generated within a comparatively short period of time. Misrepresentation must result in harm or the likelihood of harm to the wronged party.

Misuse or disclosure of confidential or secret information

It is unlawful to misuse a competitor's confidential information with a view to gaining a trade advantage.

Passing-off: copyright and rights in the get-up of the bag at left (of Commerce Afrique CC) allegedly infringed by bag at right

Passing-off: common law rights in the get-up of the original 'Rainbow' doll (at left) infringed by the copy (at right)

Copy at left infringes both the trade mark and common law rights of Dr Martins

Instances of misuse of such information are most frequently encountered in cases where a person has left an employer to start his own business, taking with him the secret information of his ex-employer – for example, customer lists, recipes, business schemes – and then proceeding to use that information in his own business. This sort of conduct has been held to be tantamount to theft and thus illegal. If the ex-employee was also a director of an ex-employer company, such conduct may also amount to a breach of the fiduciary duties of the ex-director to that company.

This position must be distinguished from that created by a *restraint of trade clause* in a contract between an employer and an employee or between two partners or shareholders in a business. Restraints of trade are aimed at preventing – or rather delaying – competitive activities that would otherwise be lawful; whereas the unauthorised use of confidential or secret information is a permanent situation until that information becomes public. Very often, however, a person subject to a restraint of trade clause may also be in possession of secret or confidential information. Because of this, restraint of trade clauses are dealt with separately below (see *Restraint of trade clauses*).

Misrepresentation about your own product

This may amount to unlawful competition where statements made about a product go beyond what is known as 'puffery' (laudatory or extravagant statements that may not strictly speaking be true, but that are not unlawful). Puffery may include statements such as 'the finest motor car in the world' or 'the best wine in South Africa'.

Other statements about a product may, however, be both untrue and unlawful. If, for example, wine that is not produced in the Champagne district of France is described as 'champagne', this would amount to an actionable misrepresentation that other traders could rely upon in instituting an unlawful competition action.

Copy at right infringes both the trade mark and common law rights of Henkel KGaA

Misrepresentation of a competitor's products or business

It is unlawful for a trader to spread untrue or malicious rumours and statements about a rival's business or products when this will lead to damage to the competitor's business. An example would be to state that a competitor's products are likely to explode and cause injury when used, if this is not so.

Breach of a statutory provision

Breach of a statutory provision by one trader, in conducting his business, may constitute unlawful competition with respect to another competing trader who is conducting his business legally.

There are many laws governing trade, including such things as having an official licence to conduct a particular type of business, or to use a particular label. In some cases, one trader operating without the necessary licence, or using a particular label, can be prevented from further trading in this way on the basis of unlawful competition. In some cases it is necessary to prove particular damages arising as a consequence of such illegal use, while in other cases, this is not necessary. It generally depends on whether the law was enacted for the benefit of the public as a whole or a particular group of people.

RESTRAINT OF TRADE CLAUSES

The term 'restraint of trade' covers clauses in contracts that aim to prevent one or both parties from engaging in certain activities for an agreed period of time after the contract comes to an end. Usually, the restraint is imposed on an employee or partner of a business, with the aim of preventing the employee or partner from competing with the other party in a similar business – for a limited period after termination of the employment or partnership.

Restraints of trade have, in the past, always been scrutinised by the Courts on the basis of whether or not they are reasonable. As in the case of unlawful competition itself, the Courts have played their part in interpreting, enforcing, or declaring unenforceable, restraint of trade clauses. The general principles that have

been developed through the Courts take into account the
fact that a contract in restraint of trade is not necessarily
wholly enforceable or wholly unenforceable. Thus a
Court could, in the public interest, order that the whole,
or only a part, or no part at all, of the restraint be
enforceable. Thus:

- The enforceability or otherwise of contracts in restraint
  of trade is a matter of public interest that depends on
  the circumstances prevailing at the 'relevant time'. The
  relevant time is usually the moment when there is an
  application to enforce the restraint. The onus of
  proving that enforcement is against public policy
  (public interest) rests on the person subjected to the
  restraint.

- A person who seeks to enforce something less than the
  whole restraint of trade specified in the contract must
  raise the issue pertinently, so that it can be dealt with
  properly in evidence and argument.

- A court is not obliged in all cases to whittle down an
  unreasonably broad restraint of trade until it eventually
  becomes reasonable. Important in this regard is the
  issue of whether or not the unenforceable part of a
  contract can be separated from the enforceable part
  without deviating from the intention of the parties, or
  creating a new contract for the parties.

- In order to be enforceable, a contract in restraint of
  trade must protect some proprietary interest of the
  person who seeks to enforce it. The Court has indicated
  that such a proprietary interest could be in the form of
  trade secrets or confidential information, goodwill, or
  trade connections.

A recent court decision

The above principles are illustrated in the case of *The
Concept Factory v Heyl* (1994 [2]SA 105TPD). In this
particular case, the relevant employee was employed for

a period of only ten months, and was responsible for the selling of advertising space in a booklet that contains an abbreviated list of businesses situated within a particular geographic area, together with their telephone numbers. The relevant part of the restraint of trade clause in issue read as follows:

> it is an express condition of employment that the employee agrees that he will not enter into competition with the employer for a period of one year within the fields of operation of the employer including the sales, publication, distribution and promotion of *The Look Guide* or any other local telephone and emergency guides to the public and businesses, within the borders of the Republic of South Africa.

After termination of the employee's employment, the employee commenced selling advertising space in a booklet that, although not identical to that of the employer, was similar to it in several respects.

In the Court proceedings instituted by the employer to enforce the above clause, the employee objected to the restraint on the grounds that it was too wide in its effect. The employer took the view, that (even if the clause was, on the face of it, unreasonable), the court could amend the unreasonable restraint to make it reasonable, and in fact confine it to the activities actually carried out by the former employer. The employer still insisted, however, that the restraint should be effective in the whole of South Africa.

The Court found that this clause was clearly intended to prohibit all competition by the employee in all the fields of activity of the employer throughout South Africa. There was no suggestion that the restraint was intended to be limited to the activities of the employer in the field of production and distribution of his own booklet. The Court stated that to enforce such a prohibition would result in the Court making a new contract for parties. The Court furthermore found that as the employer had not shown that he intended to extend his activities in connection with his booklet to the rest of South Africa, the restraint was also too wide, unreasonable, and not in the public interest. Enforcement of the restraint clause was consequently refused.

Recommendation to employers

The views expressed by the Court in this instance clearly indicate the necessity for employers to consider carefully the exact wording of restraint of trade clauses. Three main issues should be considered. Firstly, it would always be necessary to indicate that some justifiable proprietary interest of the employer is being protected by the restraint of trade clause. Secondly, the specific activity should best be limited to the exact field of activity of the employer. Thirdly, the geographical area within which the restraint would be operative must be carefully considered. Unless the employer is active within the whole of South Africa, it appears that such a restriction could be found to be unreasonable. If an employer is active only within a particular geographical area then it would appear to be advisable to restrict the restraint to that geographical area. However, the duration of the restraint should also be considered, as an unduly long period of restraint may also be problematic.

8 Product Liability and Product Warranties

PRODUCT LIABILITY

Product liability, also known as manufacturer's liability, is the manufacturer's liability for damage caused in consequence of a defective product. Damage can be purely money related, as in the case of a vehicle causing damage to property due to brake failure, or it can be non-pecuniary, as in the damage caused to a person's health by using a defective medical product.

Actions for product liability fall under the law of delict as is the case with unlawful competition. Two particular requirements of delictual actions are those of *wrongfulness* and *negligence*, thus the claimant must prove that the manufacturer caused wrongful damage and was negligent.

Wrongfulness

In order for there to be wrongfulness, there must be a defect in the product (this defect in turn leading to the damage which is the cause of the complaint). In order to determine whether a product is defective the product must be unreasonably dangerous. A product will be unreasonably dangerous if a reasonable consumer would consider it not to meet expected safety requirements, keeping in mind its ultimate intended purpose. Thus, inherently dangerous products such as razor blades cannot be seen as defective. Conversely products that have design defects would be seen as defective, including things such as: a baby's pram with ineffective brakes, which results in the pram running away and causing injury to an infant; or products carrying insufficient warnings of inherent danger.

Negligence

Having established wrongfulness it is also necessary to prove that the manufacturer was negligent. Negligence is tested on the standard of 'the reasonable man' and thus negligence is seen to exist if damage is reasonably foreseeable and could be prevented when the product is put to its normal use. It is highly advisable that these aspects, and in particular the content of instructions and warnings, be carefully considered before marketing a product. Because it is generally very difficult to prove negligence, many countries have abandoned this requirement. South Africa, however, still considers it to be necessary.

PRODUCT WARRANTIES

Warranties are commonly found in contracts, especially contracts of sale of products or other articles. Generally, warranties are viewed by purchasers as providing some form of added benefit or protection – which unfortunately may not always be the case.

In terms of the common law, the seller of goods is liable for any latent defects that may occur in the goods. Latent defects are those that existed at the time of sale and that, had the purchaser known of them, would have swayed him from entering into the contract. Where goods are found to have latent defects, the purchaser may invoke the common law 'Aquilian remedies' to obtain relief in the form of restitution, whereby the full purchase price and necessary expenses are reimbursed to the purchaser and the goods returned to the seller. Under the common law, the seller is thus liable for defects resulting from faulty workmanship or flawed materials.

Exclusion of common law remedies

However, the seller's liability for latent defects can be expressly excluded from the contract by using the so-called 'voetstoots' clause. A voetstoots clause simply means that the entire common law liability of the seller is done away with and the purchaser accepts the goods 'as they are'.

Another means of excluding common law remedies is

to set limited liability on a warranty. In the terms of a warranty, one party undertakes that a fact is as it is stated to be; or that an article is free from specified defects; or possesses a certain quality or durability. The usefulness of the warranty lies in the fact that the remedies for a breach of contract can be used if the warranty is not complied with or proves to be incorrect. If a warranty is not detailed, these remedies are difficult to invoke. When they are detailed, warranties can be powerful contractual tools whereby undertakings by one party can be made to be terms of the contract.

However, the term 'warranty' is often misused, especially in so-called 'standard form' contracts of sales, where a 'take it or leave it' attitude prevails. In such a case, the purchaser has little choice but to contract on the terms contained in the contract. Generally, in such cases, the seller warrants certain qualities pertaining to a product but simultaneously couples this with a restriction of liability on his part. To the lay person the warranty may seem rather generous, but in fact such contracts often cancel the common law remedies. Without the warranty and its statements of restricted liability, the purchaser would in fact have been automatically protected by common law against various defects in those goods.

This trade off of rights in a warranty coupled with restricted liability may appear to be fair but in fact seldom is. The purchaser usually ends up in a far worse situation with the 'warranty' than without it. The situation is amply demonstrated by the sale of motor vehicles where warranties commonly only cover certain parts of the vehicle; exclude liability for consequential loss; and endure for a limited period of time (the Aquilian common law remedies fall away only after one year). Such warranties will often also impose limitations on the purchaser by requiring certain maintenance procedures to be carried out, often only by specified parties, or the use of only specified brands of spare parts. (Clearly where certain quality standards have to be maintained these terms can be justified.)

Of a more problematic nature, however, is the question of whether or not the seller can require a certain product to be used irrespective of the quality of other products available to the purchaser. For example, a clause may state that only a certain brand of paper may be used in a photocopier where it is known that brands of equivalent or higher quality exist. The question must, unfortunately, simply be answered: 'Yes, the purchaser can be so restricted' – unless he is prudent enough to change this requirement when signing the agreement. In practice, the purchaser can achieve a lot by being careful in this regard. In other words if the warranty stipulates that a certain brand of paper for the photocopier has to be used, and the user fails to change the contract and uses a different brand, the warranty will fall away.

The legal position and the solution
It is a well established principle of our law that agreements are to be honoured. The Courts will thus generally not interfere with the terms of a contract where there has been free consent to it by both parties unless one of the parties can demonstrate some form of misrepresentation by the other party. This situation would, for example, arise where the seller of a photocopier expressly tells the purchaser that he is free to use any brand of paper before the contract is concluded, but thereafter insists on the specific brand being used if he is to honour the warranty.

It should be clear that the purchaser is in a weak contractual position in relation to the seller or manufacturer – unless considerable caution is exercised. The most effective solution to the problem appears to be one of education. Manufacturers and sellers generally want to attract and retain business. Purchasers should thus be educated to protect their rights before contracting: for example, by insisting that clauses which severely limit their rights be removed from a contract. It will be appreciated that purchasers with large buying power are more likely to succeed in this, especially where the seller has competitors, and this position should be used as a bargaining tool. The purchaser should not blindly accept the terms presented to him. The solution is summed up by the old motto *caveat emptor* or 'let the purchaser beware'.

9 Copyright

Copyright in South Africa is conferred and regulated by the Copyright Act No.98 of 1978, which came into force on 1 January 1979. It has been amended several times since then.

Copyright, broadly speaking, is the right given to the creator, author, or other person who may own the copyright of certain types of works, not to have that work copied (reproduced) without authorisation. The types of works covered by copyright are works which may be heard or seen when in a suitable form. Copyright is property and may be sold, assigned or licensed for use by others, often by way of a publication contract (as outlined under *Licences* below).

Unlike most other forms of intellectual property, copyright exists automatically and does not have to be registered. In fact, other than in the case of cinematographic films, no registration procedure is available.

WHAT IS PROTECTED BY COPYRIGHT?

Literary works

This category includes novels, stories and poetic works; dramatic works, stage directions, cinematographic film scenarios, space tooling and broadcasting scripts; textbooks, treatises, histories, biographies, essays and articles; letters, reports and memoranda; instruction manuals and advertising literature; lectures, addresses and sermons; and written tables and compilations.

Protection is not dependent on the literary quality, mode or form in which the work exists.

Computer programs and software

A computer program is specifically provided for in the Copyright Act in consequence of an amendment which became effective in 1992. A computer program is broadly defined as a set of instructions fixed or stored in any manner and which, when used directly or indirectly in a computer, directs its operation to bring about a result. It does not therefore extend to documents, data, or compilations, which are probably still protected as literary works.

Artistic works

These generally include, irrespective of artistic quality: paintings, sculptures, drawings, engravings and photographs; works of architecture (either buildings or models of buildings); technical and engineering drawings; works of artistic craftsmanship.

Musical works

Cinematographic films

These are protected in any form – whether, for instance, recorded on magnetic tape or on photographic film – so that they can be seen as a moving picture. Soundtracks of cinematographic films are also protected. Sound recordings are also protected in any form – cassettes or other tapes, compact discs, records, or any other recording medium – in which they can be reproduced in the form of sound.

Radio and television broadcasts

These are protected whether they are transmitted by radio or cable, as are programme-carrying signals.

HOW DOES COPYRIGHT COME INTO EXISTENCE?

From a practical point of view, probably the most important aspect associated with copyright is that where it exists, it does so automatically. Thus no registration is required or possible as in the case of patents, designs and trade marks. Registration is, however, provided for in the case of cinematographic films.

The requirements for copyright to exist concern the

making of the work itself, the person who made the work, and publication of the work. For copyright to exist in this country, the work must be: original; in a material form; produced by a South African or in South Africa, or in compliance with the Berne Convention; and be of a certain morally accepted nature.

Originality

The work must be original. This means that it must have been the product of the creator or author's original skill and effort, and should not be copied from another work. It does not matter that the 'idea' behind the work was not the creator's own idea or even that the work subsequently turns out to be the same as another work in existence at the time of creation, and of which the author had no knowledge. Originality basically requires that the work was the result of the creator's own effort and does not mean novelty or inventiveness, as is required in the case of patents.

Material form

The work must be reduced to a material form. This simply means that the work must exist in a tangible form such as a document, magnetic recording, or other optically, mechanically or electronically 'readable' form. Copyright cannot, therefore, exist in an idea.

Qualified person or publication

Either the creator or author of the work must be a citizen, resident or domiciliary of South Africa, or a legal body incorporated in South Africa (qualified person), or the work must have been first published, broadcast, or disseminated in South Africa.

International co-operation

Copyright also exists in South Africa in respect of works first published or created by persons who are citizens, residents or domiciliaries of, or in, foreign countries which are members of an international arrangement called the Berne Convention. South African copyright holders are similarly afforded protection in these foreign countries.

The members of the Convention include: Argentina, Australia, Austria, Belgium, Brazil, Canada, Chile, Central African Republic, Democratic Republic of Congo, Denmark, Egypt, Germany, Finland, France, Great Britain, Greece, Holy See, Iceland, India, Israel, Italy, Japan, Lichtenstein, Luxembourg, Mexico, Netherlands, New Zealand, Norway, Pakistan, Philippines, Poland, Portugal, Republic of Ireland, South Africa, Spain, Sweden, Switzerland, United States of America and Zimbabwe. (Please note that this list is not exhaustive.)

Exclusions
Copyright will not subsist in a work which is immoral, obscene, libellous or irreligious.

WHO OWNS THE COPYRIGHT?

The owner of the copyright in a work is generally the creator or author of the work. Important exceptions to this general rule include the following:

- A person who: commissions the taking of a photograph, the painting or drawing of a portrait, the making of a gravure, a cinematographic film or a sound recording; and pays or agrees to pay for it in money or money's worth, is – subject to certain provisions – the owner of any copyright subsisting in the work.

- Where a work is made in the course of the creator or author's employment by another person under a contract of service or apprenticeship, that other person is the owner of any copyright subsisting in the work.

- In the case of a computer program, the author and owner of the copyright is 'the person who exercised control over the making of the computer program'.

- If the work is made under the direction or control of the State, or any international organisation prescribed under the Copyright Act, the State or that international organisation is the owner of any copyright subsisting in the work.

- If the creator or author assigns the copyright to another person, it belongs to that person.

HOW LONG DOES COPYRIGHT LAST?

Different terms apply to different types of works, the main ones being as follows:

- literary, musical and artistic works (other than photographs) – 50 years from the end of the year in which the author of the work dies.

- computer programs – 50 years from the year in which legitimate copies were first made available to the public.

- published cinematographic films, photographs, sound recordings, radio and television broadcasts and other programme-carrying signals – 50 years from the end of the year in which the work was first published or broadcast.

- unpublished cinematographic films or photographs (not published within 50 years of the year in which they were made) – 50 years from the end of the year in which the film was made or the photograph was taken.

LICENCES

As indicated above, a copyright owner can grant a licence to one or more other persons to use the copyright on agreed terms. Where the licence is an exclusive licence (ie, the copyright owner is also precluded from using the work), the licence must be in writing. An exclusive licensee is in very much the same position as the owner of the copyright and may take legal action in connection with the copyright.

Rights of the author or owner
Copyright in – for instance – a literary or musical work,

vests in the owner of the exclusive right to reproduce the work in any manner or form. However, owners usually choose to authorise another person to reproduce the work by entering into a publication contract. Copyright in a work, however, also vests other rights in the owner, such as the right to make an adaptation of the work, which includes the translation of a literary work, the broadcasting thereof, and a conversion of the story for serialisation through pictures in a newspaper. A publication contract can therefore regulate a number of issues, including the following:

- copyright in the work itself can be assigned, partially or completely, to the publisher;

- different persons can be authorised to publish the work in different geographical areas;

- the right to translate the work or to convert the work to a script for a cinematographic film can be retained or transferred;

- the right to publish further works of the owner of the copyright can be granted;

- the publisher can be restricted from publishing competing works; and

- rights can be granted for a limited period of time.

In addition, the author of a work has the right to object to any distortion, mutilation or other modification of the work where the act complained of would be prejudicial to the honour or reputation of the author. Any such act is deemed to be an infringement of the copyright.

Rights of the publisher

The publisher of a work can have rights in relation to a work published by him that exist independently of those of the owner of the copyright in a literary or musical work. The concept of 'literary work' encompasses a number of different written works. Should publication be undertaken of a textbook, for example, the Copyright Act provides that the publisher of the work would be the author, and first owner, of the copyright in a 'published edition'. This is defined as the first print by whatever process of a particular typographical arrangement of a literary or musical work.

The typographical arrangement by the publisher of the pages of the textbook can thus confer copyright of that particular arrangement upon the publisher as opposed to the author or owner of the basic copyright. It is, however, possible to agree that such copyright would also vest in the owner of the copyright of the literary or musical work concerned.

BROADCASTING RIGHTS

South African broadcasting is being deregulated by the Independent Broadcasting Authority (IBA) and private organisations are taking over the airwaves in South Africa. The result is going to be more competition in broadcasting in South Africa. As a result, broadcasting copyright is set to become increasingly important in this marketplace.

The South African law of broadcasting is not governed by a single piece of legislation. Three Acts of Parliament create the rights and obligations of broadcasters: the Broadcasting Act No.73 of 1976; the Copyright Act No.98 of 1978; and the Independent Broadcasting Authority Act No.153 of 1993.

South Africa still has international obligations to fulfill in this regard, and there is still uncertainty about a number of provisions in the existing Acts, as they apparently conflict. The current definition of a broadcast and the rights accorded to broadcasters fall short of the requirements that South Africa undertook to provide in terms of its international obligations. It therefore appears that an amendment of the existing South African laws will have to be made at some time in the near future. This will have the effect of broadening the protection given to broadcasters in South Africa.

The Independent Broadcasting Authority (IBA) is in ultimate control over the granting of broadcasting licences. The definition of what amounts to a broadcast for the purposes of IBA regulation and what amounts to a broadcast for the purposes of copyright protection differ. For example, a satellite broadcast does technically fall within the control of the IBA, but there is no protection for foreign broadcasts in South Africa. An English soccer match broadcast to the South African public live over a satellite will thus not enjoy broadcast copyright protection in South Africa.

Nevertheless, in broadcasting copyright, as in any other form of copyright, it should be remembered that different forms of copyright can exist in the same work. For example, a feature film may have copyright in the screenplay, the cinematographic film itself, the music score and the first broadcast of the feature film in South Africa. Each of these different rights may have different owners. The mere exclusion of the broadcasting right in terms of South African law does not therefore mean that the film can be broadcast without permission from the other rights holders. In South Africa, the broadcasting right applies only to the first broadcast of the work in South Africa.

However, in some instances there are no other rights to protect a broadcaster other than a broadcasting right, such as where live events, such as sports events, are broadcast, but are not recorded by the broadcaster. Today such situations are rare, but possible.

Until 1992, the author of a broadcast was the South African Broadcasting Corporation (SABC). Since then, the author of a broadcast is whichever broadcaster is responsible for the first broadcast of the material. A broadcast is infringed if a copy of the broadcast is made, whether in the form of a moving picture, still frame or a sound recording. A broadcast is also infringed if an unauthorised re-broadcast of the work is made to members of the public. For example, if an encoded M-NET signal for a live local soccer match is decoded and distributed to a number of different television sets in a bar, the broadcasting rights of M-NET will be infringed if the M-NET broadcast was the first broadcast of that material in South Africa. However, if a person has a private party and re-broadcasts a radio signal around his home to different parts of the property, this will not be an infringement as it is a broadcast to private persons and not to members of the public.

Another way that broadcast copyright can be infringed is when a broadcast is reproduced visually or acoustically. The reproduction can be done via a loudspeaker, a radio, a television, any signal receiver or by the screening of cinematographic film or the playing of a recording, in any form, for example a CD, a record or a tape. Therefore, if a shopkeeper records music played by the National Symphony Orchestra live on SABC radio and replays it over his loudspeakers to the public, then the rights of the radio broadcaster will be infringed.

To avoid infringement of a broadcaster's copyright it is best to get a licence from the broadcaster to re-broadcast or perform its work in public. It should be remembered however, that because broadcasting is often only one of the many copyrights in any work, licences from other rights holders would also be necessary.

HOW IS COPYRIGHT ENFORCED?

Copyright entitles the copyright owner to prevent the unauthorised copying (infringement) of the relevant work by others. There is no infringement unless actual copying, at least to a substantial extent, takes place. Infringement usually takes place by the unauthorised reproduction or publishing of the relevant work, or a substantial part of it, in one way or another. In some cases (where the content of the work is more important than its actual form) infringement also takes place if an adaptation (modified form) of the work is made.

Direct and indirect infringement

It is interesting to note that infringement of copyright not only entitles a copyright owner to sue in Court for an order preventing the unauthorised person from infringing the copyright, and also for damages, but it is also a criminal offence in cases where a person imports, sells, distributes, deals in, or offers for sale, infringing works that he knows to be infringements of the copyright.

Infringement that takes place by an unauthorised person actually copying or causing the copying of a work is commonly termed *direct* infringement. Infringement by a person importing, selling, distributing, or otherwise dealing in unauthorised goods that he knows were made by an unauthorised person is commonly termed *indirect* infringement.

Plagiarism

The term 'plagiarism' sometimes refers to instances of infringement of copyright when the content, or a part of the content, of a book – or some other document that would typically constitute a 'literary work' – has been copied. Whether or not infringement has taken place is subjected to the usual test of what has been copied. It must be borne in mind that the number of pages or the extent of copyright as such is not decisive; rather the nature of the parts of the work that have been copied. It must be emphasised again here that copyright does not exist in relation to an idea. It must be noted that the term 'plagiarism' does not however have any specific legal significance, and the concept of infringement should rather be used.

'Grey' goods

The distribution of 'grey' goods, sometimes also referred to as 'parallel importation', may amount to copyright infringement in certain circumstances – even though the products involved are genuine goods. The term 'grey' goods is applied to products which are actually manufactured by the trade mark holders in one country and are imported into another country through a channel other than the official representative of the manufacturer in the importing country. Thus, although they are genuine goods, they are usually not supported by the official representative in the importing country. It is sometimes possible to prevent such 'parallel imports' by using copyright, but it is a pre-requisite that the trade mark being used on the products, the wrapping in which the products are packaged, or some other related item, must qualify for protection as a copyrighted work. A further aspect is that the copyright involved must be assigned to an entity, usually the South African representative, which is distinct from the manufacturer from which the imported article originates. This may involve assignment of the copyright to a local exclusive distributor. The date of assignment, and proof of notice of it, is of great importance in determining whether the importation or distribution of specific goods would amount to copyright infringement. In view of these requirements, it is necessary to approach the issue of grey goods with caution, and it is advisable to obtain the advice of an intellectual property law attorney in this regard.

WHICH ACTIONS DO NOT INFRINGE COPYRIGHT?

Certain actions which fall within the broad scope of protection afforded by the Copyright Act are expressly permitted and therefore do not constitute an infringement of copyright. These include:

- The use of a literary or musical work for private study, criticism or review of that work; for the reporting of current events; or any publication, broadcast or sound or visual recording used for teaching purposes. Copyright is not violated if the name of the author and the source of the extract are mentioned, and if the whole of the work, or a substantial part of it, is not reproduced.

- Reproduction of a lecture or address or other similar work which has been delivered in public, if the reproduction is for information purposes.

- Reproduction of official text books of a legislative, administrative or legal nature, speeches of a political nature or delivered in the course of legal proceedings, and news of the day that are mere items of press information.

It was formerly an infringement of copyright to copy a three dimensional article of a primarily utilitarian nature and which had been made by an industrial process from drawings thereof in which copyright existed. This process is known as reverse engineering. This type of act is no longer an infringement of the copyright in the drawings. This does not mean that copying of such articles can now be freely carried out. Great care should be taken before copying such articles as other provisions of the law may prevent it. Unlawful competition is particularly relevant (see Chapter 7). It is advisable to consult a patent attorney, agent or other specialist in the field before copying any commercial article.

HOW IS IT KNOWN THAT COPYRIGHT EXISTS?

It is not compulsory to mark works and reproductions of them to show that copyright subsists; but it is highly advisable to do so, in order to avoid innocent copying by third parties who are ignorant of the existence of copyright. Marking is generally done by printing the international copyright symbol © followed by the name of the owner of the copyright and the year in which the copyright came into existence, for example:

© John & Kernick 1998

10   The Effect of the Internet on Intellectual Property Rights

The mushrooming use of the Internet for commercial activity can pose difficult problems for commercial enterprises, particularly in relation to trade marks and copyright.

TRADE MARKS   In order to set up a presence on the Internet, a commercial enterprise must identify itself by means of a unique Internet Protect (IP) address. In its native form, an IP address is a numeric string similar to a telephone number. This type of IP address is difficult and inconvenient to use. In order to facilitate and promote Internet usage, alphanumeric aliases or synonyms are used in place of native IP addresses. These synonyms are also known as 'Internet domain names'. As the term suggests, domain names are divided up into a series of domains according to type of organisation and geographic location.

The task of registering domain names has been sub-licensed around the world to a series of domain name 'registrars'. The Foundation for Research and Development (FRD) is the ultimate South African domain name registrar. The FRD, in turn, has sub-licensed the South African domain space to a series of domain name registrars for the different types of domain names. Two examples of South African (.za) domain name types are '.co.za' (administered by Uniforum SA) for commercial organisations and '.ac.za' for academic institutions. In practice, an Internet user's service provider registers domain names with the registrars, for a fee, on behalf of their client.

The registration of Internet domain names has been largely unregulated and has operated on a first come, first served basis. It is quite possible that a business, wishing to register its business name or any of its trade marks as an Internet domain name, may find it already registered by another party. Conversely, a domain name holder may suddenly find himself in conflict with a commercial enterprise for using its business name or trade mark as part of his domain name.

In such a case a person has unintentionally registered a problematic name in ignorance of someone else's proprietary rights; or, on the other hand, the registrant foresaw a potential for profit by selling a deliberately registered domain name back to the owner of the trade mark or business name.

Mere registration of a domain name is insufficient to hold a domain name valid as there is a usage requirement. If the domain name is not regularly used by its owner within 90 days of registration, the registrar has the right to re-assign the domain name to another party wanting to use that domain name. The domain name must be regularly used after the 90-day period as well. The owner of a domain name must have a genuine intention to use the domain name.

South Africa does not, as yet, have a uniform policy for registering domain names. It appears that, whenever a dispute arises relating to a contested domain name, the registering authority prefers to suspend use of the name until the parties to the dispute have resolved their differences, either amicably or by litigation.

What can Internet users do to steer clear of any potential domain name conflicts?

• Business enterprises should seek to register their business names and trade marks as Internet domain names as soon as possible to take advantage of the first-to-register system.

• Before registration of an Internet domain name, applicants should conduct searches at the trade mark and company registries to assess the potential of name conflicts.

- Businesses should, wherever possible, register domain names as trade marks or defensive company names, or both.

- In order to satisfy the usage requirement, a domain name holder should use the domain name on a regular basis.

COPYRIGHT

Digital activity on the Internet can also often give rise to copyright related problems. A feature of the Internet is that electronic copyrightable works may appear transiently on computer screens and then disappear just as suddenly after having been in existence for just a few moments. Generally data and programs from a host Internet site are transmitted over a physical data network to an end user. The end user accesses the host site through a distribution network provided by a number of telecommunications companies and Internet service providers (ISPs). Images, animated images, video clips, text, data and sound originating from the host site may be displayed, played and stored at the end-user node and programs originating from the host site.

Further, computer programs can be transmitted from the host site to an end user, where it can be activated by the end-user. The data transmitted can be in several forms, such as contained, encrypted, compressed, packaged and real-time (such as for video clips or sound). Any data sent is also divided into smaller units, known as packets, which can be sent via the network over an extended period of time.

Copyrighted works may therefore exist transiently in different forms at different points on the Internet between the host site and the end-user. It is by no means certain that current South African Copyright Law provides adequate protection for different digital forms of otherwise copyrightable works.

ISPs are uniquely well positioned to stop the loss of

intellectual property rights on the Internet. ISPs are already promulgating and enforcing rules of usage by their customers and have suspended accounts in many instances where abuses have occurred. They can utilise and implement technology that is capable of automatically screening material on the Internet, but often the ISPs act against infringers only once notified by a complainant.

ISPs may also be liable for infringement due to any infringing activities of their subscribers. They have the right and the ability to control infringing acts and receive direct financial benefit from their subscribers' infringement of intellectual property rights.

People making copyrightable works available on the Internet should ensure that all their works bear the copyright symbol '©' followed by the year(s) of creation of the work in order to indicate that they are not in the public domain and are the subject of copyright. A notice in the works should be added which can be something to the effect that:

> This work is the subject of copyright protection in terms of the Berne Convention, other international treaties and other laws. Any unauthorised use, duplication, sale or modification of this work is strictly prohibited. All rights are reserved.

However, other non-legal ways of protecting copyright in a work on the Internet, where the works are not intended to be for general public viewing, is either to encrypt the data or to provide only limited access to the data to selected users of the Internet. There are many methods of achieving this, such as the secure sockets layer encryption provided by some 'www' servers. 'Magic cookies' can be used to identify users for future access, and works can be freely distributed in encrypted form using any number of commercial encryption software packages. Users wanting to use encrypted works must then decrypt them by supplying a key to the encrypted software and when such a key is requested, the user concerned can be identified and can also be asked to sign a non-disclosure agreement.

Proprietors of intellectual property rights should lobby for the enactment of legislation which would require ISPs to remove from their systems infringing copyright material or trade marks upon notice from a copyright or trade mark proprietor. Fortunately, recent proposals to amend the international Berne Convention on copyright, to which South Africa is a signatory, are endeavouring to improve the protection of computer-related copyright concerns, such as the protection of encrypted information and databases. It is however unclear when these amendments will be accepted and how long it will take before the members of the Berne Convention make the changes to law in their own countries.

11 Counterfeit Goods

Counterfeit goods, as in the case of counterfeit money, are goods intended to take the place of, or to make people coming into contact with them believe that they are, original products of the holder of relevant intellectual property rights.

THE CURRENT LEGAL POSITION

Most countries experience the problem of providing effective legal mechanisms to combat the distribution of counterfeit goods, which are often of a poor quality. Prior to January 1998, the protection available in South Africa was fragmented between legislative provisions dealing with copyright, and those dealing with false trade descriptions. However, a single mechanism for combating counterfeit goods was put into place by the Counterfeit Goods Act, which came into force on 1 January 1998.

Under the previous anti-counterfeit regime, the two principal statutes most often used against traders in counterfeit goods were the Merchandise Marks Act (No.17 of 1941), and the Copyright Act (No.98 of 1978).

The Merchandise Marks Act

This Act makes it an offence to:

- forge any trade mark; or

- apply to sell or sell goods with any forged or false trade mark or 'trade description' unless certain exceptional circumstances exist.

'Trade mark' in the above context refers to a *registered*

trade mark – which is another good reason for registering a trade mark (see Chapter 4). 'Trade description' is widely defined in the Act as including:

> any description, statement or other indication, direct or indirect, as to the number, quantity, measure, gauge or weight of any goods, or as to the name of the manufacturer or producer, or as to the place or country in which any goods are made or produced.

These provisions are wide ranging and aim to protect consumers against false trade descriptions. It is to be noted though, that the description must be false in a material respect: inaccurate trivialities will not suffice.

With regard to legal procedure, the South African Police Services (SAPS) require an affidavit confirming the existence of a registered trade mark, and that counterfeit goods are being sold. If the position appears to be clear, the SAPS will proceed to confiscate the goods.

The Copyright Act
In terms of this Act any person is guilty of an offence if, at a time when copyright subsists in a work, he undertakes any of the following actions without the authority of the owner of the copyright:

• makes copies of the copyrighted item for sale or hire;

• sells, distributes or hires out such an item, or by way of trade offers or exposes it for sale or hire;

• imports such an item into this country otherwise than for his private or domestic use;

• distributes such an item for any other purposes, to such an extent that the owner of the copyright is prejudicially affected; or

• purchases or acquires articles which *he knows* to be infringing copies of the work.

The procedure to be followed is firstly to inform the infringer of the copyright vesting in the particular work, in order to comply with the Act's requirement that the offence is committed only when someone is aware of the fact that his actions are an infringement. Thereafter an affidavit is supplied to the SAPS, who must obtain a warrant for the confiscation of the goods.

THE COUNTERFEIT GOODS ACT

The Counterfeit Goods Act makes it an offence to deal in counterfeit goods. Dealing in counterfeit goods occurs if any person:

- imports the goods into or through this country, or exports them from or through this country, or makes or produces goods in this country, for a purpose other than for his private and domestic use;

- possesses the goods or has them under his control in the course of business with a view to dealing in them;

- sells the goods, hires them out, offers or exposes for sale or hires or publicly exhibits them;

- distributes them for the purposes of trade; or

- distributes them for any other purpose to such an extent that the owner of any intellectual property right in respect thereof is prejudicially affected.

'Counterfeiting' means making or producing goods that imitate protected goods, so that they are a substantially identical copy of the protected goods, without the authority of the owner of any intellectual property right (subsisting in this country) in respect of the protected goods – that is, goods embodying an intellectual property right. Intellectual property rights include both rights conferred by the Trade Marks Act, and the Copyright Act, but exclude patent and design rights.

It also includes making, or applying to, goods, the subject of that intellectual property right or a colourable imitation of it, so that the goods are calculated to be taken as being the goods of the owner or to be goods made under his licence. Other specific activities are also prohibited.

PROCEDURE IN TERMS OF THE COUNTERFEIT GOODS ACT

The Act allows a complainant to lodge a complaint that someone is dealing, or is about to deal in, counterfeit goods. 'Complainant' means a person who has an interest in the protected goods, and includes the attorney, agent or representative of the owner or licensee of the intellectual property right in respect of such goods; or an importer, exporter or distributor.

The Act empowers members of the SAPS and certain other officials (inspectors) to seize counterfeit goods and to hold these goods pending the outcome of criminal or civil litigation (or both), to be instituted against the offenders. It is to be noted that whilst the Act creates a cost-effective and quick way for enabling counterfeit goods to be taken out of circulation, criminal and civil proceedings will have to be instituted by the complainant (who will normally be the intellectual property right holder) to prevent the counterfeit goods from being returned to their original owners and thus entering the market place.

Criminal proceedings are instituted when a complaint is lodged with the SAPS. The Act provides that criminal proceedings must be instituted within three days of the seizure of the goods. The SAPS investigate the matter on receipt of the complaint and the criminal investigation docket is to be sent to the relevant Public Prosecutor to decide whether to proceed with the prosecution of the party dealing in the counterfeit goods. If the Public Prosecutor proceeds with the prosecution, and if the party who dealt in the counterfeit goods is convicted, an order may be made by the Court that the counterfeit goods be delivered up to the complainant or owner of the intellectual property rights.

However, if for some reason the Public Prosecutor decides not to prosecute or the criminal court does not convict the party dealing in the counterfeit goods, it will usually mean that the counterfeit goods will be returned to the original owner. The complainant will thus be well advised to follow the criminal proceedings instituted very closely and to make representations to the Public Prosecutor if he decides not to prosecute the party accused of dealing in counterfeit goods. If there is any doubt or uncertainty whether or not the counterfeit dealer will be prosecuted, the intellectual property right holder should in any event institute civil proceedings, despite the fact that criminal proceedings have been instituted. As will be seen from what follows, the intellectual property right holder will usually only have ten court days to decide whether or not to institute civil proceedings and as the wheels of criminal justice normally turn very slowly, he will not know within these ten days whether the counterfeit dealer will be prosecuted or not.

The Act provides that the intellectual property right holder must give written notice to the person from whom the goods were seized, within ten days of the seizure, to the effect that the intellectual property right holder will institute such proceedings. The civil proceedings must then be commenced: summons must be issued or an application launched, within ten court days of the written notice. In practice, it means that the intellectual property right holder has 20 court days to prepare his case. In view of the complexity of civil proceedings in the intellectual property field, and the practical problems usually experienced with the finalising of papers, 20 court days is extremely short. It is thus advisable that before any steps are taken to have goods confiscated in terms of the Counterfeit Goods Act, that the intellectual property right holder ensures that all the documentation, information and deponents to affidavits, and any other relevant information, are readily available so that it will be possible to finalise the papers within the 20 court days.

The Counterfeit Goods Act seeks to make it easier for intellectual property right holders to have counterfeit goods confiscated and to protect their rights. Since the advent of the Counterfeit Goods Act, the old provisions used to combat counterfeit goods (particularly under the Merchandise Marks Act) have been amended to avoid areas of overlap. Bear in mind, however, that it is important to have an intellectual property lawyer involved in the whole process, to ensure first, that the counterfeit goods are not returned to the dealer, and secondly, that your rights under the Act are properly enforced.

GREY GOODS

These are not to be confused with counterfeit goods. 'Grey' goods (or as they are often termed 'parallel imports') are genuine goods originating with the proprietor of the relevant intellectual property, usually a trade mark, or an authorised licensee of the proprietor. They are, however, imported into the country by an unauthorised distributor, usually in competition with the authorised distributor.

Usually, the proprietor of the trade mark in the country of manufacture is the same as the proprietor of the trade mark in South Africa. The unauthorised importation of the 'grey' goods into South Africa is thus not a trade mark infringement. In the event that the South African distributor was the owner of the trade mark this may, on the other hand, be trade mark infringement provided the situation was not contrived for this purpose. Another possible remedy is in terms of the Copyright Act. (See Chapter 9 under *How is copyright enforced?*)

Counterfeit valve (at left) infringes trade mark of Westinghouse Air Brakes Company, and contravenes the Merchandise Marks Act by applying a false trade description

12 Plant Breeders' Rights

The protection of rights in new varieties of plants is provided for in South Africa by the Plant Breeders' Rights Act (No.15 of 1976). As new varieties of plants developed by plant breeders are unpatentable, protection for such new varieties of plants is provided for by the Plant Breeders' Rights Act. These rights enable the owner of the rights to prevent others from propagating certain new varieties of plants developed by a plant breeder.

HOW ARE PLANT BREEDERS' RIGHTS REGISTERED?

An application to register Plant Breeders' Rights is made to the Department of Agriculture and must include:

• details of the applicant;

• a description, on the prescribed technical questionnaire, as to a typical plant of the variety concerned, and the procedure to be used for the maintenance and reproduction of the variety;

• colour illustrations (black and white may be accepted), on a metric scale, of a typical plant of the variety showing characteristics of leaf, stalk and fruit or flower shape;

• an indication of the proposed denomination of the variety according to a set of rules laid down by an international union (UPOV) of which South Africa is a member; and

• details of corresponding foreign rights.

An application for registration is examined by the authorities and samples of the plant will generally be required for testing. The examination normally takes between three and five years.

Unless permission is obtained from the authorities, the variety may not be sold or commercially exploited in South Africa during the examination and until registration. Application can be made for provisional protection in order to prevent others from doing so.

NOVELTY REQUIREMENTS

Generally a variety will be deemed to be 'new' if propagating or harvested material from it has not been sold or otherwise disposed of by the breeder:

• in South Africa for more than one year; and

• in a country signatory to the Berne Convention for more than six years in respect of vines and trees, and four years in respect of all other varieties.

ENFORCEMENT OF PLANT BREEDERS' RIGHTS

It is an infringement of a plant breeder's right to sell or deal with propagating or harvested material of the protected variety without obtaining permission from the holder of the plant breeders' right. Upon proof of infringement, the holder of a plant breeders' right may recover damages from the infringing party.

HOW LONG DOES PROTECTION LAST?

Plant breeders' rights begin on the date of grant of the right and extend for 25 years in respect of fruit trees and 20 years for other varieties. An annual renewal fee must be paid every January after grant for the full term of the right. An extension of six months is available for late payment of the renewal fee.

13   Licences

One way in which intellectual property rights can be used, is to 'license' them to others. Patents, designs, trade marks, copyright, trade secrets and 'know-how' are examples of rights which can be licensed.

A licence is a means whereby a holder of rights in intellectual property, the licensor, can obtain remuneration by allowing another person, the licensee, to use his rights. The remuneration usually assumes the form of a royalty but may include an upfront lump sum payment as well. Remuneration in terms of a licence contract can assume either or both of two broad categories, namely: remuneration in money; and indirect remuneration (not money). In each of these broad categories are a number of different types of remuneration, dealt with separately below.

Ownership in the rights is retained by the licensor, as opposed to an outright sale or assignment of rights, where the ownership in the rights actually passes from one person to another. It is also possible to transfer such rights and receive a royalty based on the performance of a product which is protected by the rights. The document granting licence rights is usually referred to as a licence contract.

DIFFERENT TYPES OF LICENCES

Licences are always in the form of one of four basic types, or a combination of them.

Non-exclusive licence
This allows both the licensor and the licensee, as well as other licensees, to use the rights licensed.

Sole licence
This is similar to a non-exclusive licence, in that it allows both licensor and licensee to use the rights licensed. However, in terms of a sole licence, no other licensee may be appointed.

Exclusive licence
This allows only the licensee to use the rights licensed, and not the licensor or any other licensee.

Implied licence
This is a licence not specifically granted by the owner of the rights, but one which is, in the particular set of circumstances, an essential part of another transaction or situation. The question of whether an implied licence exists depends purely on the facts of the situation. Generally a licence can be implied where such a licence is necessary to enable all things to be done to give effect, in particular business efficiency, to a contract. The contract may be written or oral.

Some areas in which implied licences clearly exist, are the following:

• Where a custom or trade usage accepts that a licence is granted, there will be a strong implication that a licence exists unless there is a contrary indication. An example of this is where an author sends a manuscript work to a publisher of a periodical, permission to publish at the periodical's standard rates may be presumed.

• A person commissioning the making of a work in which intellectual property rights reside, may not own those rights but has an implied licence to use the resultant product. An example is where a draftsman is commissioned to do machine drawings and the person commissioning the draftsman omits to include in the contract an assignment of the resulting copyright. In this case the copyright is retained by the draftsman but the person commissioning the work is entitled to use it under an implied licence.

- Any manufacturer of products for a customer who owns intellectual property rights covering the product clearly has an implied licence to manufacture such products. The implied licence is limited only to manufacturing and not to selling the products to third parties.

REMUNERATION IN MONEY

It must be noted that there are numerous different forms of remuneration which a licensor can receive from a licensee. Each case will have its own particular set of circumstances and requirements of the licensor and licensee, and negotiations should be carried out carefully to arrive at an equitable remuneration. It must always be stressed that the remuneration must be equitable to both licensor and licensee. Also, the type of remuneration may be influenced by tax considerations. For example, if a once-off lump sum payment for an exclusive licence is contemplated, an outright sale may be better for the licensor, as this 'capital' payment may be tax-free if handled correctly.

Once-off lump sum payment

A licensee can be required to pay a licensor a single payment of money for the right to use the technology for a predetermined length of time or, alternatively, forever. In this case both the licensor and licensee run substantial risks. The licensor risks that use of the relevant technology may make substantial amounts of money – in which case the licensor could have benefited to a greater extent from some other arrangement, for example a running royalty. On the other hand, the licensee's use of the technology may be totally unsuccessful – in which case the lump sum is lost to the licensee.

Initial down payment

An initial down payment is often made by a licensee to a licensor simply for the right to obtain the licence, and is usually coupled to one of the forms of royalty payments or licence fees mentioned below. The down payment is usually non-refundable and may be regarded as a sign of good faith on behalf of the licensee. Such a payment also serves the very practical purpose of reimbursing the licensor for costs incurred in development of the relative technology and any costs of procuring intellectual property protection for the technology. In the case of exclusive licences (in which the technology holder is precluded from use of the technology in competition with the licensee) the lump sum payment is often regarded as compensation to the licensor for divesting himself of the right to use the technology. Sometimes a down payment is treated as an advance on royalties, in which case it is recovered by the licensee as royalties are earned in terms of the licence contract.

Annual licence fee

In some cases it is extremely difficult to measure the extent to which licensed technology is being used, simply because of the nature of the technology. For example, a method of ore-dressing a mineral may not bear any relationship to the quantity of product finally produced. In such cases it is often regarded as appropriate to charge a single licence fee per annum which may be escalated over a period of time in accordance with a predetermined formula.

Running royalties

By far the most common form of remuneration is the running royalty which is often combined with a down payment. A running royalty is related to the extent of use of the technology by the licensee. A running royalty may therefore be based on any of the following factors:

- A percentage of the manufacturer's selling price (in 'arms-length' transactions to customers other than affiliated companies) after deduction of taxes, duties, transport costs, etc. Such a basis puts the obligation on the licensee to keep full sales records, and provides a practical and effective way of calculating royalties. This is generally the most common, and least troublesome, basis.

- The number of items sold in a predetermined royalty period (often quarterly).

- The nett sales value of products of the licensed technology. The total turnover in a predetermined licence period.

- The savings relative to a particular datum.

- Any other suitable basis.

It must be noted that profits are generally not used as a basis for royalty payments as the profit can be too easily manipulated or affected by mismanagement or other factors.

Extent of royalties

The extent (or quantum) of the royalties is a matter for negotiation. As a very general guideline there has been conceived a rule, called 'the 25% rule', in terms of which the licensor would be entitled to 25% of the perceived benefit of the use of the technology by the licensee. The perceived benefit may take various forms and, in the case of a new product, could simply be the profit the licensee should make. It may, alternatively promote sales of other non-patented products thus giving the licensee increased profits. It may thus extend a product range of the licensee. The benefit could be the savings in the case of a manufacturing process.

Royalties generally amount to between 1% and 10%, based on the manufacturer's selling price, and usually fall between 2% and 7%. Factors influencing the extent of the royalty payment would generally include the following:

- the total extent of the benefits;
- the nature of the technology;
- the exclusivity or otherwise of the licence;
- the territorial extent of the licence;
- the licensor's ongoing liability to enforce or defend the

relevant intellectual property rights;
* the licensee's risks;
* the duration of the licence;
* the development work required of the licensee.

Generally a *minimum* royalty payment will be required yearly, possibly as from the second or third year of operation of the licence contract, simply to ensure that the licensee actually uses the licence, or otherwise terminates it. A licence should not be allowed to obstruct use of the technology, and a minimum royalty or other performance clause should be sufficiently onerous to make it impractical, from a business point of view, to pay the minimum royalty whilst not using the licence. On the other hand the minimum royalty or other performance provision should be realistic and achievable.

The terms of payment of royalties and any other monetary payments in terms of a licence should be set out clearly in the licence contract.

INDIRECT REMUNERATION

A licensor can derive additional or alternative benefits from the grant of a licence in various ways that do not involve the direct payment of money. The following are some forms of non-monetary remuneration.

Equity or joint venture
The licensor may be given shares in an existing company or, alternatively, the licensor could contribute the technology to a joint venture with the licensee contributing, say, the manufacturing facility.

Tied sales
The agreement may provide for the licensee to purchase from the licensor certain commodities – either related or unrelated to the licensed technology – to the advantage of the licensor. In this respect, care should be exercised where a patent is being licensed, as the South African Patents Act restricts the licensor from reserving for himself the right to supply non-patented articles to the licensee, other than spare parts or the like for a machine

falling within the scope of the licensed patent. In addition, a patent licence may not restrict the licensee from using any unpatented process; may not fix resale prices; and may not restrict the licensee from selling the patented product in any country where the product is not patented.

Equipment lease

The licensor may lease equipment to the licensee, in particular equipment for using the licensed technology, and the lease payments may be sufficient to remunerate the licensor for the licensee's use of the technology.

Cross-licence

It may be that the licensee is in possession of technology which the licensor would like to use. In such a case the remuneration received by the licensor could be a licence from the licensee to use such technology. The cross-licence may simply be a non-royalty payment arrangement or may be combined with royalties, generally at a lower rate than would otherwise be paid.

THE LICENCE CONTRACT

A licence takes the form of a contract, which may be oral or in writing. When concluding a licence contract in terms of which royalties are to be paid to a foreign licensee it is important to remember that approval of the Exchange Control Authorities must be obtained before the agreement is signed.

The following are some of the more important points which should be considered when negotiating a licence contract:

- the nature of the licence, for example, whether it is a non-exclusive, sole, or exclusive licence;

- exactly what technology is being licensed;

- whether the validity of the intellectual property being licensed has been investigated;

- the territory in which the licence is effective;

- the right of the licensee to grant sub-licences;

- the transferability of the licensee's rights;

- the type and quantum of remuneration payable to the licensor and the method of payment;

- the duration of the licence;

- regarding termination of the licence, the circumstances under which the licensee or the licensor may terminate the licence, especially in view of inadequate performance by the licensee;

- who owns the rights in improvements relating to the basic rights, and whether or not these automatically fall into the licence;

- who will enforce or defend the rights licensed;

- which law is applicable in international licences; and

- any preferred dispute resolution procedures between the parties.

REGISTRATION OF LICENCE CONTRACTS

Some agreements, such as patent licence contracts and trade mark registered user agreements, should preferably be registered at the Patent and Trade Mark Offices if the full benefits of the agreement are to be obtained.

Great care should be taken in drafting licence contracts and professional assistance from a patent attorney or other expert in the field should be obtained.

14 Franchising

Franchising is really a sophisticated form of licensing. It has a highly developed form, widespread application and, consequently, considerable economic significance.

Whilst there is generally no accepted definition of a franchise (either locally or internationally), it usually involves the provision by a franchisor, to a franchisee, of a substantially complete business package in return for a payment. This payment is usually related to the turnover of the franchise operation and will often include an initial lump sum payment. A franchise will enable the franchisee to conduct a business which supplies goods or services of a particular character, without requiring any ingenuity or special business acumen on the part of the franchisee. The business will usually be financed by the franchisee, but there are many instances in which the franchisor may become financially involved in the business.

A look at the definition of a franchise as put forward by the International Franchise Association is also helpful:

> The franchise operation is a contractual relationship between the franchisor and the franchisee in which the franchisor offers, or is obliged to maintain continuing interest in, the business of the franchisee in such areas as know-how and training; wherein the franchisee operates under a common trade mark, format or procedure owned or controlled by the franchisor, under which the franchisee has made, or will make, a substantial capital investment in his business from his own resources.

Common examples of successful franchises are the well-known fast food and clothing chains. There are also many service chains, particularly in the communications and printing industries, that are extremely successful.

THE FRANCHISE AGREEMENT

All franchises are controlled by a franchise agreement which sets out the rights and obligations of both parties. This agreement will control the relationship between the two parties for the entire duration of the franchise, and it is thus as well to ensure that it is acceptable to the licensee and that no hidden pitfalls are present. As these agreements are often extremely complicated, it is almost always advisable to consult a legal adviser, such as an intellectual property practitioner. It can also be extremely enlightening to talk to other existing franchisees involved in the same chain.

There are two main components in a franchise agreement: the business package; and the payment made to the franchisor.

The business package

This generally includes all information and necessary licences to enable the franchisee to commence business under the format of the franchisor. The following features are generally included, to whatever extent is appropriate:

• A licence to use the franchisor's trade marks.

• A licence to use the franshisor's trading get-up and style. This includes the type, design, and colouring of the premises.

• If any patents or registered designs are involved, the licence to use these.

• Information to support the requirement that certain production, processing, and marketing procedures and standards are followed and maintained in the conduct of the business; and an undertaking to fulfill this requirement.

- The supply of certain literature and any essential stationery formats applicable to franchisees generally by the franchisor.

- The requirement that specified accounting procedures be followed.

- The obligation that the franchisor be responsible for necessary training of the franchisee and staff.

- The requirement that the franchisee purchase certain commodities from prescribed sources, often the franchisor (such requirements have to be kept within legal limits).

- The obligation on the franchisor to promote the product or service on a global or regional front by advertisements or otherwise.

- A restriction on the franchisee as to the area or market sector that he is permitted to address, or in which he is permitted to operate. The franchise will often be in respect of a particular building or business centre.

The payment to the franchisor
The payment to the franchisor in consideration of the rights and information supplied to the licensee is normally quite simple in that it usually consists of:

- An initial lump-sum payment for the rights and information granted.

- An ongoing royalty or commission based on either the gross turnover in money terms, or the extent of business conducted by the franchisor, as measured in some other way.

PROTECTING A FRANCHISEE – THE DISCLOSURE DOCUMENT

In order to protect over-enthusiastic franchisees from becoming bound to a franchise agreement in the heat of the moment, the South African Franchise Association, a body of which most reputable franchisors are members, requires the preparation of a Disclosure Document. This document must formally advise a prospective franchisee of the following:

• the nature of the structure of the franchisor;
• the officers of the franchisor;
• details of the franchise being offered;
• the obligations of both parties;
• the financial obligations of the franchisee; and
• information about other current and past franchisees.

The Disclosure Document enables a prospective franchisee to consider the venture properly, within a given period, and thus to avoid becoming bound to an agreement whose obligations he cannot adequately meet.

THE ADVANTAGES OF A FRANCHISE OPERATION

To the franchisee

The franchisor provides the franchisee with all the necessary information for setting up and running the franchise operation including, very often, building, décor, and floor-plan designs; information about suppliers of necessary or recommended hardware and fittings as well as suppliers of stock and consumables not supplied by the franchisor; recipes and other information about running the business; and, very often, information about management, record keeping and accounting procedures to be followed. The franchisee and his staff will often even receive necessary training from the franchisor.

The franchisee becomes a part of a larger whole and benefits from the reputation, development, and improvement of the overall business to which the franchise relates. It is a 'small fish with a big fish ability' in a restricted area.

The exact package will vary from one franchise operation to another. Some franchise operations are so well developed and complete that the franchisor may prefer to appoint a franchisee with no previous experience of running his own business.

To the franchisor

The main advantage of franchising to the franchisor is that each franchisee, whilst working for his own advantage, is building up the goodwill which is owned by the franchisor. It is this goodwill itself that is the attraction to other prospective franchisees. A series of franchisees can build up this goodwill more quickly than could the franchisor himself.

The franchisor acquires input from many different sources – that is, the various franchisees – and this input can be put to the common ongoing purpose of all franchisees and the franchisor.

Mutual advantage

Statistics have shown that out of all new businesses that start up (not including franchise operations), about nine out of ten fail during the first ten years, whilst in the case of franchise operations, this figure is only about one or two out of ten.

15 Managing and Using Intellectual Property Assets

The intellectual property rights discussed in this book are tools that are applied in business. They can be expensive, and acquiring them will require your time and resources. If you are acquiring more than the odd intellectual property right, it is important to consider how you will administer them, and manage their use. Intellectual property rights are assets in your hands, and we refer to them as intellectual property assets.

Time is always at a premium at management level, but to maximise the effectiveness of your intellectual property rights, appropriate time and resources must be devoted to administering and managing your intellectual property. This should be done at the highest level an organisation can afford, and from a position that has insight into the working end of the product or service covered by the intellectual property rights.

Strategic use of intellectual property rights requires an understanding of intellectual property law and its application in the product or service life cycle. To take a simple example, patents and designs require filing at the inception of a new product or the rights are lost. At the same time, there are dangers in delaying the filing of an application for the registration of a trade mark, even though such application need not be made prior to using the trade mark.

Sadly, patent and other intellectual property practitioners only too often see a client simply because the client finds itself in a conflict over rights, or under threat from competitors. The correct time to check for potential difficulties, and to maximise your intellectual

property protection, is at the commencement of an
innovation exercise. This applies irrespective of whether
the innovation is of a technical nature, or a new franchise
operation that is to be launched. The checklist set out
here indicates the kind of opportunities and threats that
should be taken into account prior to launching a
technical innovation. (See p115–121.)

**A GENERAL
COMMENT ON TAX**

As regards the tax status of intellectual property, it is
clear that intellectual property is in the hands of its
creator. Usually the product of his business activity (and
therefore the source of taxable income – is also in his
hands, and may, under certain circumstances, constitute a
capital asset. For example, an author would be taxed on
the sale of the copyright in his books; an inventor on the
royalties derived from licensing out the manufacturing
rights to articles patented by him, and they would
accordingly be entitled to claim the deductions and
allowances outlined here in the *Innovation Launching
Checklist.*

On the other hand, someone who does not make a
business of inventing, writing or composing may
nevertheless acquire (or even himself create) something
that attracts some form of intellectual property rights. He
may then proceed to exploit his invention or work,
earning income in the form of direct profits or a derived
benefit, such as royalties, from it. He thus holds the right
itself as a capital asset, and is entitled to regard any profit
on its eventual sale as a capital gain – even though the
income from it was taxable while he held the right.

Even if someone holds an item of intellectual property
as a capital asset and does not derive any income from it
during a specific year of assessment, this does not
preclude him from claiming the allowances provided for
in the Income Tax Act – in regard to the development,
acquisition, and so on, of the right in question – as
deductions from his overall taxable income.

Another point to bear in mind is that income derived
from intellectual property, whether by direct exploitation
or as royalties, licence fees, and so on, is taxable at

source. This has been held to mean the place where the right is exploited or from which the royalty emanates – irrespective of where the holder of the right (or the licensee or other exploiter) may be domiciled, or of where the agreement in question was concluded.

These considerations can be important in taking advantage of the provisions of the Act relating to the imposition of foreign taxes, in view of the relatively high rates of taxation applicable to income sources in South Africa.

Never neglect to claim the tax deductions to which you are entitled!

MONITOR THE INTELLECTUAL PROPERTY PORTFOLIO

Your intellectual property assets, like any other assets, should have their performance tracked against cost, and an assessment made. Intellectual property rights should therefore be recorded against a product or service, and not filed as a separate entity according to some unconnected file reference. You cannot, of course, assess an intellectual property right unless you know what strategic purpose it was put to in the first place, or to what product or service it applies.

Similarly, intellectual property rights should be reviewed annually, at the same time as the business that the intellectual property rights support, is reviewed. If this is done, you can make a sensible decision on whether to renew or lapse an intellectual properly right, or acquire new intellectual property rights in conjunction with fresh business innovation. A decision to renew intellectual property rights may be made without any intention of using them offensively, but purely for the purpose of inhibiting – or at least delaying – the use of their subject matter by others. Remember that a trade mark registration can be cancelled on the ground of five years' continuous non-use, and compulsory licences under patent can be obtained under certain circumstances.

If your intellectual property rights include a portfolio of international rights, you will be faced with quite heavy expenses in the form of prosecution fees and, later, annual renewal fees throughout the world. These expenses can be properly managed only if you regularly assess the performance of the intellectual property rights and the product performance and expectations in a particular country.

There are many ways in which proper management of, and insight into, the use of an intellectual property portfolio can benefit an organisation. For example, much can be learned from examining a company's intellectual property rights portfolio. Take a situation where standard products have been sold for many years, coupled with ageing or expired intellectual property rights: this indicates a company trading in the downswing of a product life cycle. In South Africa, such a company often has one staple product and a few minor ones, which it has produced for many years in a standard industry, such as the mining industry. If such a company is suddenly faced with an innovative competitive product, or a straight copied product coupled with price competition, the result can be very damaging indeed.

Proper use of intellectual property rights can provide and maintain a competitive edge for the company that understands these rights and can manage them.

INNOVATION LAUNCHING CHECKLIST

1 The Defensive List

The first set of rights to check are those that may clash with your venture, and that would allow someone else, possibly a competitor, to take legal proceedings against you and inhibit or prevent your exploitation of the innovation. We divide this list into rights that are registered, and thus can be searched for and found, and a second category of rights that are unregistered.

REGISTERED RIGHTS

Patents

Do a general technology and infringement search as soon as the innovation is nearing the stage where it could be technically defined. This ensures that exercising the invention commercially will not infringe an existing patent. The results of such a search could lead to a different approach or variation of the technology being used or developed, in order to avoid infringement. A search at this stage might also help to assess the novelty of the innovation and may provide valuable information as to the state of development of the particular technology concerned, so you can avoid 're-inventing the wheel'. When investigating the possibility of infringement, always remember that patents are territorial in effect, so that you must clear yourself of infringement, if necessary, in every country in which you intend the innovation to be used.

Trade marks

You should always select a trade mark with great care, and clear it of possible conflict with other registered trade mark rights. Preferably also clear it as far as possible against other lists of trade names, such as commercial directories, and companies and close corporation registries. The costs and difficulties involved in having to change a trade name after its launch can be enormous. These include having to destroy and replace – even recreate and rename – costly pamphlets, brochures and stationery, and also to retrieve and destroy any products manufactured, packaged, and possibly already in the market place under an offending name. As with patents, bear in mind that trade marks are for the most part territorial, and that clearance in South Africa will not mean that the trade mark is available for your use in foreign jurisdictions.

Designs
The possible infringement considerations for design rights are much the same as for patents. Remember in this case, however, that in countries overseas there may be common law design rights that do not fall within the scope of a registered right. Generally speaking, the chance of infringing someone else's registered or unregistered design right, if your innovation is entirely original, is remote. It is in instances that you have attempted to emulate or compete with an existing product that great care should be taken in this regard.

UNREGISTERED RIGHTS

Copyright
Copyright is not a common law right but exists in terms of the Copyright Act. Nonetheless it is an unregistered right in South Africa, and in most other countries of the world. Check whether you are possibly infringing any copyright. If to your knowledge you have not copied anything in the production of your innovation, you cannot infringe copyright. If on the other hand you have used materials – such as printed matter of others – in order to create your own materials, you should obtain a professional opinion as to whether or not the extent of your 'copying' will constitute an infringement. In addition, if you have employed or contracted other people to do work for you in creating your materials, you must be sure that the work, or any components of it, do not infringe the copyright of others. This is often difficult – if not impossible – to establish, because you will not be able to ascertain whether or not those persons used unauthorised matter, for example from a proprietary computer image database. Your solution here is to get contractual indemnities from such persons, and

always to employ or contract only with reputable people or organisations.

Unlawful competition

Be aware of the possibility of falling foul of the law of unlawful competition. If you have obtained information from any person during the course of negotiations, or under the cloak of any form of confidentiality or contractual undertaking, you must be careful how this information is used. If it includes designs or market related ideas and the like, seek advice about the extent to which you may utilise such information or ideas. Also, beware if you are attempting to copy existing products in order to share in a good market that has been generated by one or more others. Whilst copying a product that is not protected by any registered or unregistered rights is, on the face of it, legal, great care must be exercised to ensure that the products – and in particular, the manner in which you propose to sell and promote them – do not offend any established rights of others.

Product liability

Ensure that your products are of acceptable standard and do not create any unnecessary danger to any user or other member of the public. If the product is inherently dangerous ensure that adequate and appropriate warnings are given.

INNOVATION LAUNCHING CHECKLIST

2

The Offensive List – Opportunities

Many intellectual property rights are lost if they are publicly exposed before protection has been applied for. In some cases rights are lost because their origin is not established, and arrangements are not made contractually to take transfer of all the necessary rights.

**REGISTERED
RIGHTS**

Patents
It is essential to decide whether you are going to apply for patent protection *before* you publicly expose your invention. If you feel the need to do limited marketing or technical testing beforehand, it is best to obtain a secrecy undertaking, preferably in writing, from *every* person who will be exposed to the invention. You can also consider doing novelty or other searches at this stage to test the validity of any possible patent that you might obtain for your invention.

Registered designs
The shape of certain elements, or their appearance, may be capable of protection by a design registration. Although, from the time that you first issue the design, you have a six-month grace period in which to file a design application, it is far preferable to file a design application before publicly exposing it.

If you expose your invention before filing, it will prevent you from *patenting* the invention; but you can still apply for a *registered design* if you do so within six months of the date of the public launch of the design. However, be careful about delaying filing such a registered design application until after launching the design – because you will be unable to stop a third party from manufacturing and marketing copies of your design, after your launch, but before you file your registered design application. Also, you may have destroyed your rights to file in at least some foreign countries.

Trade marks
It is not a legal requirement that you apply for registration of a trade mark before the mark is used or becomes known, but early filing of the application will assist in maintaining your ownership of the mark, and result in easier enforcement after registration is granted.

Trading / company / close corporation name
If you are setting out on a new business venture, give serious consideration to registering it as a company or close corporation – and preferably give it a name embodying your trade mark, in order to protect it fully. If this is not possible (or you wish to avoid, for instance, using a multiplicity of trade marks under a general brand name), consider defensive name registrations. (See Chapter 5.)

Always remember: trading as a company or close corporation has the effect of limiting your public liability if something should give rise to a claim resulting from the conduct of your business.

UNREGISTERED RIGHTS

Disputed ownership of copyrights can cause serious difficulties for innovators especially where they have contracted out services or have used employees to produce works. Obtain the necessary assignments in writing, of *all* intellectual property rights, especially of copyright, from *all* contractors and parties who may create rights whilst doing work for which you are paying.

The question of ownership
In the case of a large company or organisation there is seldom any question about ownership of any intellectual property rights. (The company – or sometimes a holding company, or even an offshore entity – is often used as the owner of the rights, depending on the circumstances.) However, the position of small companies, close corporations, and one-man businesses is often quite different.

Where a single person or small group of people conduct a business by way of a company or close corporation, and gain a particular item of intellectual property (such as a patent for an invention they have made), it is in their interest to handle ownership of the right correctly: they may acquire a capital gain, and the accompanying tax advantage through doing so. This is done by registering the right (usually a patent) in the name of the person or persons (usually the inventor or inventors); and allowing the company or close corporation to use the right. Such a right may in this way increase in value, and the owners can then sell the right to the company or close corporation for a capital sum. Clearly this can be done only once, or once every now and again, as the revenue authorities may otherwise decide that the person concerned is trading in innovation – in which case the purchase price paid becomes fully taxable. Of course, all royalties are taxable in any event if a royalty-earning relationship is chosen. The same principles apply if an inventor deals with a totally independent licensee or purchaser.

Tax deductions

Once again the large company or organisation will have a policy of ensuring that the optimum tax deductions are obtained in connection with all expenses incurred in the process of securing, maintaining and enforcing intellectual property rights, as well as in any defence against attacks on the validity of the rights by others. However, for those who are not familiar with the current position in South Africa, the following tax deductions can generally be claimed in respect of any of the above types of costs incurred in the course of business, or with a view to deriving income from any intellectual property rights that may be secured. The situation may vary in relation to time, changes in the law, and specific circumstances, so you should, at the outset, get the advice of a competent tax consultant in any specific case. The following serves as a guide:

• Costs of general *legal advice* or opinions in connection with intellectual property rights: Fully deductible in the relevant tax year.

• Costs of *registering* intellectual property rights: Technically the costs of acquiring any intellectual property rights should be written off over the useful life of the relevant intellectual property right. It is always extremely difficult to judge the extent of the useful life of such a right and it is quite common for the tax authorities to allow the total cost to be deducted in the year in which the costs are incurred, even though this is not strictly correct, in most cases.

- Annual renewal or *maintenance fees*: Fully deductible in the relevant tax year.

- Costs of *enforcing rights* against others: Logically, these should be fully deductible in the relevant tax year, being costs incurred in protecting a market. However, this may not be viewed in the same light by the tax authorities. Such costs should be claimed, and if disallowed should be negotiated with the tax authorities.

- Costs of *defending intellectual property rights* against attack by others: Similar to enforcing rights, except that there is the added danger that the tax authorities may view these costs as relating to a defence of property, and therefore as not deductible. Again, negotiate with the tax authorities if a claim to these costs is disallowed. The costs of *defending your business* against the attack by others on the basis of their intellectual property can be dealt with in a similar way.

- Costs of *research and development*, prototypes, models, tools, dies, jigs, etc, are also deductible – in certain cases, in the form of depreciation. The larger organisation or specialist research organisation automatically claims all allowable deductions; the small company and individual inventor should also look at this very carefully. Often deductions that are not immediately apparent can be claimed.

16 The Law of Contract

Commerce and the Law of Contract go hand in hand. Although the latter is an indispensable and complex part of everyday business, it is often neglected. A basic knowledge of the Law of Contract is crucial to every business person. This chapter is aimed at giving a brief and basic description of the general principles of the Law of Contract in South Africa, looking at two broad areas: the requirements for the formation of a valid contract; and remedies that are available in the case of breach of such a contract.

REQUIREMENTS FOR THE FORMATION OF A VALID CONTRACT

Capacity to contract

Any party to a contract, whether a natural person or a legal entity, must have the capacity to enter into that specific contract. All natural persons are freely entitled to enter into any agreement, with the exception of a minor, someone who is mentally handicapped or under curatorship, and anyone demonstrably under the influence of alcohol or other substances. In the case of a company or other legal entity, a duly appointed or authorised official or representative must contract on its behalf.

Legality

Another requirement is that the contract and its purpose or the performance to which it relates must be lawful (ie, not contrary to legislation or to the public interest or good morals). A distinction is usually made between agreements that are void as a result of illegality and agreements which, although valid, are unenforceable.

Restraint of trade clauses may apply in certain

circumstances. These clauses refer to the restriction, under a contract, of a person's legal capacity to partake in specified economic activities, including a trade or profession. Our courts have refused to enforce restraints of trade (whether partially or otherwise) where it was felt that to do so would be against public policy. However, in view of recent decisions of the Constitutional Court the law on this point is currently rather unsettled.

Formalities

'Formalities' refers to the outward form of the contract. There are a number of statutes in South Africa which require formalities in respect of a wide range of different contracts. These include contracts relating to the sale and purchase of immovable property, the granting of credit, long term lease agreements, suretyship agreements, mineral lease agreements, and others – in addition to those specifically mentioned elsewhere in this book.

Contrary to what many people believe, in all other circumstances, an oral contract is *binding*. However, proving an oral contract is, in the absence of special circumstances, extremely difficult, if not impossible. Accordingly, it is advisable to reduce the contract to writing, to facilitate proof of the terms of the agreement, should this become necessary. Where a contract has been written down, cognisance must taken of the rule in our law which is generally referred to as the 'parol evidence rule'. This rule was described by the Appeal Court as meaning that when a contract has been reduced to writing, the writing is generally regarded as the exclusive memorial of the transaction, and in a suit between the parties no evidence to prove its terms may be given save the document or secondary proof of its contents. In addition, the contents of such a document may not be contradicted, altered, added to or varied by parol (that is, oral) evidence. This rule is however subject to various exceptions.

Possibility of performance

The performance to which a contract relates must be

possible at the time of conclusion of the contract. An objective test is applied, and if it is found that the performance was in fact impossible, the agreement will be regarded as null and void from the start.

Consensus

The basis of any contract is agreement – a meeting of the minds of the contracting parties – which is generally referred to as consensus. Such consensus must be externally manifested and must relate to a performance with economic value. The parties must further have a conscious intention of being bound by the contract and must be aware of its consequences. Consensus is often affected by factors such as mistake, misrepresentation, duress and undue influence. It naturally follows that either the formation or the continued existence of the contract will be affected by these factors.

One interesting exception to this is when a mistake relates to a party's motive for entering into the contract. For example, A buys a new house in the mistaken belief the he inherited a large sum of money the previous day. If this turns out not to be so, he will nevertheless still be bound by the agreement, as his own motive for entering into the contract is not relevant.

Offer and acceptance

As stated above, the consensus of the parties must be outwardly manifested. This usually refers to an offer by one party and the acceptance of the offer by the other party. Thus, where the offer is withdrawn prior to acceptance or where the offer is rejected, no contract will have been formed. An offer which is accepted subject to certain conditions is regarded as a counter-offer which, in order for consensus to be present, must be accepted by the party who made the original offer.

REMEDIES IN CASE OF BREACH OF CONTRACT

The law affords a contracting party three different remedies in the case of a breach of contract by the other party: claim for specific performance; cancellation of the agreement; and a claim for damages. A claim for damages is available irrespective of whether the contract is cancelled or upheld. The contracting parties may however decide to facilitate *potential* claims for specific performance, cancellation or damages, by reaching consensus on the remedies for breach of the contract in advance.

Specific performance

This is generally referred to as the natural remedy for a breach of contract, because it accomplishes what the contracting parties initially intended. The aim of this remedy is to prevent injustice and to uphold public policy. Specific performance usually takes the form of a claim for the payment of an agreed amount, the rendering of obligations (for example service), or an injunction to order the party to refrain from certain actions which it agreed not to do. The Court has discretion as to whether to order specific performance.

Cancellation

The right to withdraw from a contract is an extraordinary remedy, and is not automatically available to an aggrieved party to a contract. Contracting parties often agree on the circumstances under which either party will have the right to cancel the agreement. If this has been done, the party who wishes to withdraw is not obliged to do so, but may choose to maintain the agreement and claim specific performance. A decision to cancel the agreement must be communicated to the other party and contracts usually provide how this is to be done: for example, notice periods, addresses of service, and so on.

Repudiation is one example of a circumstance that may entitle a party to withdraw from an agreement. Repudiation is a form of breach which usually involves one party who is trying to withdraw from the contract by notifying the other party that he cannot or will not perform. Repudiation is also present where a party disputes the terms of the contract or fails to perform his obligations properly in terms of the contract.

Cancellation results in the termination of the parties'

obligations under the contract. The parties to a contract have the right to restitution (returning the position to what it was before the contract existed) in the case of cancellation – unless it is impossible or inequitable to do so, in which case the question of damages may be relevant.

Damages

The purpose of an award of damages is to place the claimant in the position in which he would have been, had the other party not breached the contract. In this regard a distinction must be drawn between a contract that contains a penalty clause and one that does not.

The following principles are applied when claiming damages in the absence of a penalty clause:

- The claimant must prove that he has in fact suffered damages, and demonstrate the extent of the damages.

- The aim is to place the claimant in the position in which he would have been had the breach not been committed.

- Any gains that the claimant may enjoy as a result of the breach, are also taken into consideration.

- There must be a factual cause or connection between the breach and the damage.

- The claimant will have no claim if he could have prevented the damages through the exercise of reasonable care. Further, the claim is limited to damages that the parties had indeed foreseen, or that they are presumed to have foreseen.

- The claimant is entitled to damages that can be assessed in monetary value only. Personal damages may not be claimed on the basis of a contract.

- The claimant is entitled to claim an amount of money

only as damages, and damages are awarded only once.

Parties to a contract may agree on the payment of a sum of money in the event of a breach of contract. Such a clause is referred to as a penalty clause and obviates the need to prove the extent of damages that may be suffered. The Conventional Penalties Act (No.15 of 1962) regulates penalty clauses and stipulates that such a clause is enforceable unless the penalty is out of proportion to the prejudice suffered by the aggrieved party. In such a case the Court may reduce the penalties to the extent it may consider equitable in the circumstances.

Index

advantage, unfair 10, 42, 50, 61
advertising 44, 62, 66, 73, 108
African Regional Intellectual Property
  Organisation 30
Aquilian remedies 69
ARIPO *see* African Regional Intellectual
  Property Organisation
artistic works 13, 74
assignment of rights 10, 16, 23, 55, 73, 83,
  98, 99

Berne Convention 75–6, 88, 89, 97
blueprints 37
branding 12, 40, 43
Broadcasting Act 79
Business Names Act 53, 54

Close Corporation Act 52, 53
close corporations 11, 52, 119
  name 12, 52–4
Commissioner of Patents 28
common law 12, 13, 40, 45, 46, 48, 51, 61,
  62, 69, 70
Companies Act 52, 53–4
company 10, 11, 13, 20, 21, 23, 46, 52, 58,
  63, 103, 114, 122
  name 12, 52–53, 54, 87
  registry 87
competition, unlawful 10, 12, 13, 61–7, 68,
  84, 117
computer programs 9, 10, 13, 17, 37, 74, 76,
  77, 87
Concepts Factory v Heyl 65
confidential (secret) information 9, 38, 62–3,
  65
Constitutional Court 123

contracts *see also* licences
  breach 124
  employment 13, 23, 63–6
  law of contract 122–7
  oral 123
Conventional Penalties Act 127
copyright 9, 10, 13, 14, 61, 62, 73–84, 85,
  87, 88, 89, 90, 91, 95, 98, 112, 116, 119
  assignment 99
  exclusions 76
  infringement 78
  ownership 76–7
  requirements 74–5
Copyright Act 73, 77, 79, 83, 87, 90, 91, 92,
  95, 116
  amendment 74
copyright symbol '©', 84, 88
counterfeit goods 12, 90–5
Counterfeit Goods Act 90, 92, 93–4
Court of the Commissioner of Patents 26, 28
courts *see* legal action
criminal offence 49, 51, 82, 93, 94

damages 28, 29, 38, 46, 59, 60, 61, 62, 64,
  82, 97, 124, 126, 127
databank, database 19, 22, 89, 116
defensive name 52, 53, 54, 87
delict, law of 61, 68
designs 9, 57, 58, 59, 60, 68, 107
  aesthetic 12, 57
  functional 56
  registered 7, 9–10, 12, 39, 55–60, 116,
    118
Designs Act 12, 55, 56, 57, 58
disclosure 23, 108–9
dispute resolution 105

drawings 13, 23, 33, 55, 58, 74, 84, 99

employee 9, 13, 23, 63, 64, 65, 66
Exchange Control Authorities 104

field of invention 32
films (cinematographic) 13, 14, 73, 74, 77
foreign jurisdictions 18, 20, 21, 24, 30, 50, 60, 75, 76, 96, 104, 113
formulae 37
Foundation for Research and Development 85
franchise 10, 14, 106–10, 112
    agreement 107
    disclosure document 108–9
franchisee 46, 106, 107, 108, 109, 110

geographical limits 30, 66, 67, 78, 85, 108, 109
'grey' goods 82–3, 95

income tax, 9, 100, 112–113, 120–1
Income Tax Act 112
Independent Broadcasting Authority 79–80
Independent Broadcasting Authority Act 79
infringement 19, 28, 29, 31, 82
    copyright 78, 80–4, 88, 92
    patent 35, 36, 115
    plant breeding 97
    registered design 59
    search 20, 21, 29
    statutory 49
    trade mark 40, 45, 46, 49–50, 95
    trading name 52
innovation 9, 10, 14, 31, 33, 112, 113
Innovation Launching Checklist 115–21
integers 34–5
intellectual property rights *passim*
    expiry 114
    international 113
international
    assets 113
    agreements 30, 41, 44, 50, 60, 75, 79, 88, 89, 96
    licence 105
    organisations 76, 77
    searches 19, 30

International Convention of Paris 30, 41, 44, 50, 60
International Franchise Association 106
Internet 14, 85–9
    copyright 14, 53, 85
    domain name 53, 85, 86, 87
    encrypted data 87, 88, 89
    IP (Internet Protect) address 85
    ISP (Internet service provider) 85, 87, 88, 89
    legislation 89
    trade marks 85
IP address *see* Internet
ISP *see* Internet

'know-how', 11, 37–9, 106
    expiry 39
    transfer 38

legal action 15, 21, 26, 28, 44, 50, 54, 58, 59, 61, 65, 66, 68, 77, 81, 86, 93, 94, 115, 123, 125, 127
'Letters Patent' document 26
liability
    limited 70
    manufacturer's 68
    product 13, 68–9, 117
    warranties 13, 68, 69–72
licence *see also* franchise
    compulsory 28, 59–60, 113
    contract 10, 11, 14, 16, 37, 38, 39, 50, 55, 73, 98, 101, 103, 104, 106, 112
    cross-licence 104
    exclusive 77, 99, 100, 101, 104
    expiry 39
    implied 99, 100
    non-exclusive 98, 99, 104
    sole 99, 104
licensee 38, 39, 46, 50, 77, 93, 95, 98, 99, 100, 101, 102, 103, 104, 105, 107, 108, 113
literary works 13, 73, 99
litigation *see* legal action
logo 11

M-NET 81
manuals 37
marketing schemes 37
Merchandise Marks Act 90, 95

misrepresentation 64, 71, 124
monopoly 15, 33, 34, 35, 55
musical works 13, 74, 79, 80, 81

operating instructions 37

passing-off 13, 44, 51, 62
patent 7, 9, 10, 11, 12, 14, 15–30, 31–36, 38,
    39, 84, 103, 105, 111, 113, 115, 118
  amendments 26
  application 25
  attorney or agent 10, 15, 25, 30, 34, 35, 36
  database 19
  expiry 15, 27, 31, 33, 39
  family search 21
  full patent 11
  inventiveness 19
  name index search 19, 20
  novelty 17
  patentability search 21
  petty patent 11
  records 20
  revocation 26
  searches 18, 19–22
  specification 11, 15, 18, 23–27, 29, 30,
    31–35
  subject matter search 21
  utility 18
  validity 35
Patent Co-operation Treaty 30
Patent Journal 25, 26, 47, 48
Patent Office, South African 16, 19, 23, 25,
    26, 27, 29, 105
patent offices, foreign 19, 22, 29
Patents Act 15, 16, 18, 24, 26, 27, 28, 103
pictures 13, 55, 58, 78
piracy 9, 12
plagiarism 82
plans, technical 13, 37
plant breeders' rights 9, 14, 96–7
Plant Breeders' Rights Act 14, 96
police see South African Police Services
prior art 22, 32
product liability see liability
product warranty see warranty
public domain 37, 38, 88
public policy 65, 123, 125
publication contract 73

'puffery' 63

radio broadcasts 74, 79–81
recipes 37
registered designs see designs
Registered Designs Office 60
registered trade mark, symbol ®, 49
Registrar of Companies 54
release date 57, 58, 59, 60
remedies, legal 40, 53, 69–70, 122
remuneration, forms of 10, 11, 38, 59, 98,
    100–5, 106, 108
restraints of trade 9, 47, 61, 63, 67, 122–3
reverse engineering 84
royalty 10, 11, 28, 38, 59, 98, 100, 101–3,
    104, 108, 113
  extent (quantum), 102
  minimum 103
  running 100, 101

secret information see confidential information
software see computer programs
sound recordings 13, 77
South African Broadcasting Corporation 80
South African Police Services 91, 92, 93
state of the art 57
statutory provisions 40, 50, 51, 64, 90, 123

technology
  licensing 11, 100, 101, 102, 103, 104
  patenting 11, 17, 31, 34
television broadcasts 74, 79–81
trade description 91
trade marks 7, 9, 10, 11, 12, 14, 40–50, 53,
    54, 60, 61, 62, 74, 82, 85–91, 95, 98,
    105, 106, 107, 111, 113, 115–6, 119
  abbreviation, TM 49
  attorney or agent 10, 45
  cancellation 48
  'class' 46–7
  foreign protection 46
  opposition 48
  registered trade mark, symbol ®, 49
  registration 40
  renewal 48
  searches see Trade Marks Register
  TM 49
Trade Marks Act 40, 42, 44, 47, 53, 92

Trade Marks Office 46, 105
Trade Marks Register (searches) 45, 48, 50, 86
trading name 12, 45, 51, 52, 53, 119
trustee 46

unfair advantage *see* advantage, unfair
unlawful competition
   see competition, unlawful

video recordings 14
voetstoots clause 69

warranty, product 68, 69–72
www servers 88